Parables & Wisdom from the Apocrypha

Sirach, Odes of Solomon, and Other Hidden Classics of Moral Insight

A Modern Translation

Adapted for the Contemporary Reader

Various Ancient Writers

Translated by Tim Zengerink

Table of Contents

Preface - Message to the Reader

What If You Could Help Rebuild the Greatest Library in Human History?

Thousands of years ago, the Library of Alexandria stood as the crown jewel of human achievement — a sanctuary where the collected wisdom of every known civilization was gathered, preserved, and shared freely.

And then, it was lost.

Through fire, conquest, and the slow erosion of time, humanity lost not just books — but ideas, dreams, discoveries, and stories that could have changed the world forever.

Today, the Library of Alexandria lives again — and you are invited to be a part of its restoration.

Our mission is simple yet profound:

To rebuild the greatest library the world has ever known, and to translate all timeless works into every language and dialect, so that no seeker of knowledge is ever left behind again.

By joining our movement to rebuild the modern Library of Alexandria, you become part of an unprecedented mission:

- **Unlimited Access to the Greatest Audiobooks & eBooks Ever Written:**

  Instantly explore thousands of legendary works—Plato, Shakespeare, Jane Austen, Leo Tolstoy, and countless more. All instantly available to read or listen, placing a complete literary universe at your fingertips.

- **Beautiful Paperback & Deluxe Editions at Printing Cost**

  Own any title as an elegant paperback, deluxe hardcover, or stunning collectible boxset—offered to you at true printing cost, delivered straight to your door. Build your personal Library of Alexandria, crafted for beauty, built for durability, and worthy of proud display.

- **Fresh Translations for Modern Readers—in Every Language & Dialect**

  Enjoy timeless masterpieces reimagined in clear, contemporary language—no more outdated phrases or obscure references. Alongside the original versions, we're tirelessly translating these classics into every language and dialect imaginable, ensuring accessibility and understanding across cultures and generations.

- **Join a Global Renaissance of Literature & Knowledge**

  You directly support expanding our library, publishing deluxe editions at true cost, translating works into all global languages, and bringing humanity's greatest stories to people everywhere. By joining today, you're not just preserving a legacy of masterpieces; you set in motion a powerful wave of literary accessibility.

Become a Torchbearer of Knowledge.

Join us for free now at **LibraryofAlexandria.com**

Together, we will ensure that the light of human wisdom never fades again.

With gratitude and a shared love of knowledge,
The Modern Library of Alexandria Team

Visit:

www.libraryofalexandria.com

Or scan the code below:

Introduction

The Hidden Wellspring of Ancient Wisdom

Throughout history, humanity has turned to sacred texts not only to understand divine revelation but also to glean insight into how one ought to live. Beyond prophecy and theology, ancient scriptures also offered ethical blueprints, poetic encouragement, and meditative instruction. While the canonized Bible continues to inspire billions, many luminous voices remain just beyond its official boundary—part of the Apocrypha and Pseudepigrapha—speaking in tones rich with compassion, discipline, and spiritual resilience.

This collection, Parables & Wisdom From the Apocrypha, gathers the enduring moral teachings, hymns, and reflective poetry found in books like Sirach and The Wisdom of Solomon, as well as lesser-known gems such as the Odes of Solomon, The Psalms of Solomon, selected Testaments of the Twelve Patriarchs, and The Sentences of Sextus. Each of these works serves as a polished fragment of wisdom carved from the greater mosaic of ancient Judeo-Christian reflection.

The texts selected for this volume span centuries and cultures. Though some were written in Greek by Hellenized Jews, and others were composed by early Christians influenced by Jewish tradition, all share a common aim: to shape the soul through reverent devotion and righteous conduct. These writings were cherished by generations of faithful readers, cited by Church Fathers, and embraced by communities seeking spiritual maturity. While doctrinal disputes and ecclesiastical boundaries eventually led to their exclusion from many Bibles, their teachings remained hidden in plain sight—preserved in liturgy, commentaries, and devotional practice.

Today, in an age marked by ethical confusion, technological overload, and existential longing, the messages of these texts are perhaps more vital than ever. Their meditations on integrity, mercy, humility, and reverence toward the divine speak to universal human questions. They don't just prescribe belief; they model how to live well. In the Psalms of Solomon, we hear the sorrow of a people longing for justice. In the Odes of Solomon, the soul rises in song toward divine light. In Sirach and the Wisdom of Solomon, practical and philosophical teachings merge with poetic reverence. The Testaments of the Patriarchs remind us of generational legacy, while the sayings of Sextus condense ethics into brief, piercing wisdom. Each text invites the reader to slow down, reflect, and live more attentively.

Sirach, Wisdom, and the Path of Ethical Living

Among the most celebrated of the apocryphal wisdom texts, Sirach (also called Ecclesiasticus) and the Wisdom of Solomon function as a spiritual guide for those who seek to walk righteously. Written in the centuries before Christ, both books represent the culmination of Jewish wisdom traditions, offering instruction on how to lead a just and reverent life in an often hostile and idolatrous world. Sirach's author, Jesus ben Sira, draws from the Book of Proverbs but enriches it with deeper ethical and social reflection, speaking extensively on the duties of children to parents, humility before God, and the dangers of wealth, pride, and gossip. Its vivid imagery and practical tone resonate across cultures and epochs.

In contrast, The Wisdom of Solomon stands at the confluence of Jewish tradition and Hellenistic philosophy. It explores divine justice, the fate of the soul, and the nature of true immortality. It wrestles with profound questions: Why do the wicked prosper? What is the reward of the righteous? Its teachings emphasize that wisdom is not merely intelligence or learning, but an active, divine presence—one that accompanied God at creation and continually guides those who seek truth.

Together, these texts form the philosophical and theological spine of apocryphal wisdom. They confront human suffering and injustice not with simple answers but with a call to steadfast virtue, humility, and trust in divine order. Though their origins lie in a tumultuous historical period—marked by oppression, exile, and cultural tension—their insights feel timeless.

Hymns, Testaments, and the Poetry of the Soul

Complementing these philosophical works are poetic texts that pulse with spiritual longing and sacred beauty. The Odes of Solomon and Psalms of Solomon represent the devotional and liturgical core of Jewish and Jewish-Christian communities in the Second Temple and early Christian periods. The Odes, in particular, are remarkable for their language of divine intimacy. They celebrate God as a fountain of joy, a liberator of captives, and a source of radiant light. Their emphasis on transformation—of death into life, sorrow into song, captivity into freedom—mirrors the themes found in New Testament writings, though often voiced with even more lyrical grace.

The Psalms of Solomon, meanwhile, reflect a community seeking righteousness amid political upheaval and foreign domination. Likely composed after the Roman conquest of Jerusalem, these psalms lament the loss of the Davidic line while also looking forward to a coming Messiah. Their spiritual urgency and psalmic style provide an emotional bridge between the canonical Psalms and later Christian hymnody.

Alongside these poetic works, this collection includes select passages from the Testaments of the Twelve Patriarchs, which offer fatherly counsel from Jacob's sons. Though written pseudonymously, these texts preserve layers of inherited wisdom—urging repentance, fidelity, forgiveness, and love. They underscore the moral duties that bind generations and define the identity of a covenant people.

The Sentences of Sextus, one of the earliest compilations of Christian-ascetic wisdom, adds a final thread to this tapestry. Its succinct maxims are reminiscent of Proverbs or Desert Fathers' sayings, designed not to be analyzed but to be lived. Each sentence offers a distillation of virtue, encouraging vigilance, restraint, gentleness, and gratitude.

These diverse voices do not contradict each other. Rather, they harmonize in their shared call to moral clarity and spiritual depth. They invite us to listen—not just to the words of prophets or priests, but to the whisper of wisdom itself. The wisdom that builds homes, repairs communities, and awakens souls.

Let this collection serve not only as a literary and historical resource but as a guide for your own journey. May its verses illuminate your path, its counsel soften your heart, and its songs stir your spirit toward love, truth, and holy wonder.

Sirach (Ecclesiasticus)

The Wisdom of Jesus, Son of Sirach, also called Ecclesiasticus, is a collection of wise teachings and practical advice. It was written by Jesus, son of Eleazar, son of Sirach, a devoted Jewish scribe. Originally written in Hebrew between 200 and 175 BCE, the book was later translated into Greek by his grandson. It reflects a deep connection to Jewish law, history, and faith.

Sirach covers many important topics, including respect for God and how to build good relationships with others. It offers guidance on living a moral and meaningful life, showing that following God's commandments is the key to being a good person. In the translator's introduction, the book's purpose is explained: to preserve and share this wisdom across different cultures and generations.

As one of the deuterocanonical books, Sirach was included in the Septuagint and remains part of the Apocrypha in many Christian traditions. Known for its poetic language and practical advice, this book offers timeless lessons that help people strengthen their faith and navigate daily life.

The Wisdom of Jesus
the Son of Sirach (Ecclesiasticus)

Many important teachings have been passed down to us through the law, the prophets, and the writings of those who came after them. These lessons have given Israel great wisdom and guidance. It is not only important for people to learn and understand, but also for those who love knowledge to share it with others—both by speaking and writing.

My grandfather, Jesus, spent his life studying the law, the prophets, and the writings of our ancestors. Through his dedication, he gained deep understanding and felt inspired to write a book that would offer wisdom and guidance. His goal was to help those who love learning grow in wisdom and live according to the law.

I ask you to read this book carefully and with an open mind. If some parts of the translation do not fully capture the original meaning, please be understanding. Words that were first written in Hebrew sometimes lose their full meaning when translated into another language. This is true not only for this book but also for the law, the prophecies, and other writings, which are richer when read in their original form.

When I came to Egypt in the thirty-eighth year of King Energetes' reign, I found a copy of this book filled with valuable teachings. I believed it was important to translate it and share it with others. With great care and effort, I worked for a long time to complete this translation and publish it. My hope is that those living far from their homeland will also find it useful as they seek to learn and live according to the law.

Chapter 1

All wisdom comes from the Lord and stays with Him forever. Who can count the grains of sand on the shore, the drops of rain, or the endless days of time? Who can measure the sky above, the earth below, the depths of the sea, or the vastness of wisdom?

Wisdom was created before everything else, and understanding has always existed. Who has found where wisdom begins? Who has fully understood her deep knowledge? There is only one who is truly wise and worthy of great respect—the Lord. He created wisdom, observed her, and measured her. He spread wisdom across all He created and freely gives her to those who love Him.

Respecting the Lord brings honor, joy, and happiness. It is like a crown of celebration. It fills the heart with delight, brings gladness, and leads to a long life. Whoever fears the Lord will receive His favor, be blessed at the end of life, and be honored when it is time to leave this world.

Respect for the Lord is the beginning of wisdom. It is planted in the hearts of faithful people, even before they are born. Wisdom has built a strong foundation among humans, and her trust remains with their children. Respecting the Lord brings a life full of wisdom's gifts, and her rewards bring peace and contentment. She fills homes with treasures that are valuable and storerooms with blessings.

The fear of the Lord is the crown of wisdom. It brings peace and good health to all who follow her ways. The Lord measured wisdom and poured out knowledge and understanding. He gives honor to those who hold on to her. Respect for the Lord is the foundation of wisdom, and from it grows a long and fulfilling life.

Uncontrolled anger leads people to make mistakes and stumble. A patient person may struggle for a while, but joy will come in time. A wise person knows when to speak, and many will respect their words.

A wise saying is like a treasure kept safe with wisdom, but a sinner rejects what is good. If you want wisdom, follow the commandments, and the Lord will give it to you freely. Respect for the Lord brings wisdom and instruction, and He is pleased by faith and humility.

Do not turn away from the fear of the Lord, and do not approach Him with a divided heart. Do not pretend to be righteous in front of others if your heart is not sincere.

Be careful with your words. Do not lift yourself up too high, or you might fall and bring shame upon yourself. The Lord will reveal your secrets if you have not lived with true respect for Him. No dishonest heart can ever be hidden from Him.

Chapter 2

If you choose to serve the Lord, be ready to face challenges. Stay strong, be patient, and don't panic when trouble comes. Stay close to Him and don't turn away, so that in the end, you will be blessed. Accept any hardships that come your way, and stay patient when you feel brought down. Just like gold is purified in fire, people who are worthy are tested through struggles and suffering. Trust in Him, and He will support you. Follow the right path and put your hope in Him.

All of you who respect the Lord, wait for His mercy and don't turn away, or you will fall. Those who fear the Lord should trust Him, because your reward is guaranteed. Hope in the Lord for good things, eternal joy, and His mercy.

Look back at the stories of those who lived before you:

- Has anyone ever trusted in the Lord and been let down?
- Has anyone who stayed loyal to Him been left behind?
- Has anyone who called out to Him been ignored?

The Lord is full of kindness and mercy. He forgives sins and rescues people when they are in trouble.

But trouble will come to those who are fearful and weak, to those who hesitate between right and wrong. Trouble will also come to those who lack faith, because they won't be protected. And trouble will come to those who give up too soon—what will you do when the Lord comes to judge you?

Those who respect the Lord will follow His words. Those who love Him will live by His ways. Those who fear Him will try to please Him. Those who love Him will obey His commands. Those who fear the Lord will prepare their hearts and humble themselves before Him.

We choose to put our trust in the Lord rather than in people. His power is great, and so is His mercy.

Chapter 3

Listen to me, my children, as a father speaks to his family. Follow my advice so you can live safely. The Lord has given fathers respect over their children and given mothers authority over their sons. Whoever respects their father will have their sins forgiven, and whoever loves and honors their mother is like someone collecting valuable treasures. If you honor your father, you will find joy in your own children, and your prayers will be answered. Respecting your father will bring you a long life, and listening to the Lord will bring happiness to your mother.

Treat your parents with the same respect you would show a leader. Honor your father through your actions and words so that his blessing will be upon you. A father's blessing builds a strong foundation for his children's lives, but a mother's curse can bring them ruin. Do not take pride in your father's shame, because his dishonor does not bring honor to you. A person's dignity is tied to how they treat their father, and a mother's disgrace brings shame to her children.

Support your father as he grows older, and do not make his life difficult. Even if he starts to lose his understanding, be patient with him and do not disrespect him just because you feel stronger. The kindness you show your father will not be forgotten and will count in your favor instead of your mistakes. When you go through struggles, this kindness will be remembered, and your sins will disappear like frost melting in the sun. Abandoning your father is like rejecting God, and those who upset their mother will be judged by the Lord.

My child, live humbly, and you will be loved by those who are worthy. The more important you become, the more humble you should be, and the Lord will bless you. His power is beyond measure, and He is honored by those who live with humility.

Do not chase after things that are too hard for you to understand or try to figure out things beyond your ability. Focus on what the Lord has commanded, because you don't need to know everything. Do not worry about things that are too complicated, as God has already revealed more than you could ever fully understand. Pride has led many people to destruction, and their wrong beliefs have caused them to make foolish choices.

Just as you need eyes to see, you need knowledge to have wisdom. A stubborn heart will lead to trouble, and those who go looking for danger will eventually suffer because of it. A hard-hearted person will be weighed down by their struggles, and sinners will add more sins to their load. Prideful people cannot be healed because their wickedness has taken deep root.

A wise heart understands lessons, and a wise person values those who listen. Water can put out a burning fire, and helping others can make up for past mistakes. Those who give generously focus on what truly matters, and in their time of need, they will find help.

Chapter 4

My child, don't take away what a poor person needs to survive or make someone in need wait longer than necessary. Don't make a hungry person feel worse, and don't upset someone who is already struggling. Don't add to the pain of someone who is grieving, and don't delay when someone asks for your help. Never ignore someone who is suffering or turn your back on a poor person who comes to you. If someone asks for help, don't refuse them, and don't give anyone a reason to curse you. If a person cries out in frustration, God, who created them, will hear their prayer.

Respect your community and show humility to those in leadership. Listen to the poor and speak to them with kindness and patience. Help those who have been treated unfairly, and don't hesitate to stand for justice. Be like a father to orphans and a protector to widows, and you will be seen as a child of the Most High. He will love you even more than your own mother does.

Wisdom strengthens those who seek her and supports those who follow her. Whoever loves wisdom loves life, and those who search for her will find happiness. Staying close to wisdom brings honor, and the Lord will bless those who walk with her. Serving wisdom means serving the Holy One, and God loves those who love her. Those who listen to wisdom will have influence, and those who follow her will live in peace. If someone trusts in wisdom, they will inherit her, and their children will benefit from her as well.

At first, wisdom may lead a person through difficult times, testing their heart and challenging their soul with discipline. She will correct them and push them to grow. But once she sees that they are truly committed, she will guide them on the right path, bring joy into their life, and reveal her secrets to them. However, if they turn away from her, she will let them fall on their own.

Pay attention to opportunities and stay away from evil. Don't be ashamed to protect yourself. Some shame leads to sin, but other shame brings honor and kindness. Don't show favoritism to the wrong people, and don't lower yourself just because you are afraid of others. Speak up when necessary to protect yourself and others, and don't hide your wisdom to avoid upsetting people. A person's wisdom is shown by their words, and their knowledge is revealed by how they speak.

Don't go against the truth, or you will embarrass yourself with your ignorance. Don't be afraid to admit when you're wrong, and don't resist doing what is right. Don't let foolish people take advantage of you, and don't give special treatment to the powerful. Stand for the truth, even if it costs you everything, and the Lord will defend you.

Think before you speak, and don't be lazy in your actions. Don't act like a tyrant at home, and don't be overly suspicious of those who serve you. Don't be quick to take from others but slow to give back when it's time to repay.

Chapter 5

Do not depend on your wealth or say, "This is all I need." Do not follow your own desires or use your strength to chase after whatever your heart wants. Do not think, "No one can tell me what to do," because the Lord will hold you accountable.

Do not say, "I've done wrong, but nothing bad has happened," because the Lord is patient. Do not take forgiveness for granted and keep adding sin upon sin. Do not say, "God is always merciful, so He will forgive all my mistakes," because He is both merciful and just. His judgment will come upon those who continue to do wrong.

Do not wait to turn to the Lord. Do not keep putting it off, thinking you have plenty of time. His judgment could come suddenly, and you may be caught unprepared. Do not put your trust in dishonest wealth, because it will be useless when trouble comes.

Do not follow every new trend or go along with everything others do. That is the way of a dishonest person. Be firm in what you know is right, and let your words be thoughtful and trustworthy. Be quick to listen but slow to respond, speaking only after careful thought.

If you have wisdom, share it with your neighbor; but if you lack understanding, it is better to remain silent. Words have the power to bring either respect or disgrace, and a person's own speech can lead to their downfall.

Do not be known as someone who spreads gossip or uses words to hurt others. Just as a thief faces shame, those who speak dishonestly will face judgment.

Do not ignore anything, no matter how small or unimportant it may seem.

Chapter 6

Don't turn against others and become an enemy instead of a friend. A bad reputation brings shame and embarrassment, and those who lie or deceive will suffer because of it. Don't be arrogant or let your pride destroy you like a wild bull. Pride drains your strength, ruins your success, and leaves you empty like a dead tree. A wicked heart will slowly eat away at a person, making them a joke to their enemies.

Kind words help you make many friends, and showing respect earns admiration. Stay on good terms with many people, but only trust a few with your deepest secrets. If you want a real friend, test them in hard times before trusting them too quickly. Some people are only around when life is good but disappear when things go wrong. Others act friendly but later turn against you, causing trouble and shame.

Some people will gladly share your food and home, but when problems arise, they will leave you behind. When things are going well, they will act like they belong in your house, even ordering your servants around. But in bad times, they will betray you and disappear. Stay away from enemies, but even with friends, be cautious.

A true friend is like a strong shelter, as valuable as a rare treasure. No amount of money can buy a real friend because their worth is beyond measure. A loyal friend is like a healing medicine, and those who honor the Lord will find such a friend. People who fear the Lord will choose their friends wisely, because their friendships will reflect their character.

My child, seek wisdom early, and it will stay with you throughout your life. Search for wisdom like a farmer plants crops—be patient, and you will enjoy the harvest. The effort you put in will be small compared to the reward. To those who don't understand, wisdom may seem too difficult, and those who lack patience will give up on it. At first, wisdom may feel like a burden, but once you truly accept it, it will lead you to success.

Wisdom doesn't reveal herself to everyone, but she shows her true nature to those who seek her. Listen to me, my child, and follow my advice. Don't reject my guidance. Hold onto wisdom, even when it seems challenging at first. Be patient and don't resent the lessons she teaches. If you chase after wisdom with all your heart, she will show herself to you, and once you find her, never let her go.

In the end, wisdom will bring you peace and fill your heart with joy. Her lessons will strengthen you, and her guidance will bring honor to your life. Wisdom will be like a golden decoration and a royal robe, wrapping you in glory and happiness.

If you truly want to learn, you will. If you open your heart, wisdom will come to you. Love to listen, and you will gain knowledge. Pay close attention, and you will become wise. Spend time with elders and stay close to those who have wisdom. Listen eagerly to every good lesson, and don't ignore words of understanding. If you meet someone wise, seek them out early and visit them often.

Let your thoughts focus on the Lord's commandments, and reflect on His teachings. He will strengthen your heart, and your desire for wisdom will be fulfilled.

Chapter 7

Stay away from wrongdoing, and it will stay away from you. Turn away from evil, and it won't bother you. My child, don't plant the seeds of wickedness, or you'll harvest nothing but trouble. Don't demand greatness from the Lord or seek special honor from a king. Don't try to justify yourself before God, and don't show off your wisdom in front of powerful people.

Avoid becoming a judge if you're not ready for the responsibility, or you may struggle to correct injustices or let fear of the powerful influence your decisions. Don't sin against your community or bring shame upon yourself in public. Don't repeat your mistakes, because even one wrongdoing will be remembered. Don't think, "My many offerings will make up for my sins." Instead, come before God with a humble heart.

Don't be lazy in prayer, and always be generous to those in need. Never mock someone who is suffering, because the same God who humbles can also lift up. Don't lie about your brother or deceive your friend. Speak truthfully, because lies only bring harm. When you're among wise people, don't try to dominate the conversation, and when you pray, avoid meaningless repetition.

Respect hard work and farming, for they are part of God's plan. Don't surround yourself with sinners, remembering that God's judgment always comes in time. Be humble, for the wicked will face destruction. Don't trade a true friend for money or a loyal brother for wealth. Treasure a wise and kind wife, for her goodness is worth more than gold.

Treat a hardworking servant with fairness and kindness; don't take advantage of those who work for you. Value a wise servant, and if they prove themselves worthy, don't deny them their freedom. If you own animals, take good care of them; if they serve you well, be responsible for them. If you have children, teach and guide them early so they learn to be disciplined. Care for your daughters' well-being, but don't spoil them.

Choose a wise and good man for your daughter to marry, and you will have fulfilled an important duty. If you have a good wife, cherish her and don't push her away. But be cautious with those who show cruelty. Honor your parents with all your heart, and remember everything they have done for you. Think about how they raised you and brought you into this world, and consider how you can repay even a small part of their love and sacrifices.

Honor the Lord with all your heart, and show respect to His priests. Love your Creator with all your strength, and never turn your back on His servants. Fear God and give His priests their rightful share, including first fruits, offerings, and sacred gifts. Be generous to the poor so that your blessings will be complete.

Kindness and generosity bring favor, so don't hold back from helping others, even those who have passed away. Comfort those who are grieving and mourn with them. Don't hesitate to visit the sick, for these acts of kindness will build love and goodwill. In everything you do and say, keep eternity in mind, and you will avoid sin.

Chapter 8

Avoid arguing with someone in power, or you might end up under their control. Don't debate with a rich person, or they might use their wealth against you—money has led many people astray, even kings. Don't get into a fight with someone who loves to argue, and don't add to their anger—it's like adding wood to a fire.

Don't make fun of someone who has no respect for others, or you might bring shame to your own family. Don't judge someone who has changed their ways—remember, we all have made mistakes. Don't insult an elderly person, because one day you'll be old too. Don't celebrate when someone dies—death comes for everyone.

Don't ignore the wisdom of those who are experienced. Learn from their teachings—they will guide you and help you understand how to act around important people. Don't overlook the lessons of the elderly; they learned from those before them. Their words will help you grow in wisdom and teach you how to handle difficult situations.

Don't provoke a sinner, or you may get caught up in their anger. Don't challenge a rude person, or they may trap you with their words. Don't lend money to someone more powerful than you, but if you do, be ready to lose it.

Don't make promises you can't afford to keep, and if you do, be prepared to face the consequences. Don't take legal action against a judge, because the court will likely side with them out of respect for their position. Don't travel with a reckless person—they will only bring trouble. Their selfish and foolish behavior could put both of you in danger.

Don't fight with an angry person or go with them to dangerous places, because they don't value life. If trouble comes, they will abandon you and leave you to face it alone.

Don't seek advice from a fool—they won't know how to help you and won't keep your secrets. Don't share personal matters with a stranger—you never know what problems it could cause. Be careful not to open your heart to just anyone, and don't expect everyone to treat you with the same kindness you show them.

Chapter 9

Don't let jealousy take over when it comes to the wife you love, and don't teach her anything that could come back to harm you. Don't give your strength to a woman or let her control your life. Stay away from prostitutes, or you might fall into their trap. Avoid spending time with a woman who sings to entertain, as her charm could easily draw you in. Don't stare too long at a young woman, or you might get yourself into trouble. Don't give your heart to prostitutes, or you could lose everything you've worked hard for.

Don't wander the streets without a purpose or hang out in lonely places. Turn your eyes away from a beautiful woman, and don't focus too much on looks. Many have been led astray by beauty, as desire can burn quickly like fire. Don't eat or drink with a married woman, or you might start feeling attracted to her, leading to disaster.

Don't abandon an old friend because no new friend can fully replace them. A new friend is like fresh wine—it only brings real joy once it has aged. Don't be jealous of the success of sinful people, because you don't know how their lives will end. Don't take pleasure in the temporary happiness of the wicked. Remember, they won't escape judgment.

Stay far away from anyone who has the power to take a life, and you won't have to live in fear of death. If you must deal with such a person, be careful not to make a mistake that could cost you everything. Always remember that life is full of risks, like walking along the edge of a city wall.

Whenever you can, get to know your neighbors, and seek advice from wise people. Talk with those who understand what's right, and focus your conversations on the teachings of the Most High. Share your meals with good and righteous people, and let your true pride come from your respect for the Lord.

A skilled worker earns respect for their craft, just as a leader is honored for their wisdom. A loud and boastful person is a danger to their community, and someone who speaks carelessly will always be disliked.

Chapter 10

A wise judge teaches and guides his people, and a good leader keeps his government running smoothly. Just as a judge's character influences those he rules over, the way a leader governs affects the behavior of his people. A careless and reckless king can destroy his nation, but a wise ruler helps his city grow strong. It is the Lord who decides who rises and falls, placing leaders in power at the right time. True success comes from the Lord, who gives honor to those who seek wisdom, like a hardworking scribe.

Don't hold onto anger against your neighbor for every little mistake, and don't respond to others with violence. Both God and people dislike pride and arrogance. Nations lose their strength and fall apart because of injustice, greed, and cruelty. How can someone made from dust and ashes be proud, especially when our bodies start to decay even while we are still alive? Long illnesses remind us that even doctors have limits, and even the greatest kings today will face death tomorrow. In the end, all that remains of a person are bones, worms, and decay.

Pride begins when someone forgets about the Lord and turns away from the One who created them. It leads to sin, and those who hold onto it will bring trouble upon themselves. This is why the Lord has brought down the proud and removed them completely. He takes rulers off their thrones and replaces them with humble people. God uproots nations and replaces them with others. He tears down lands to their very foundations and wipes out some nations so completely that they are never remembered again.

Pride was never meant for people, and anger was not intended for human beings. Who deserves true honor? Those who respect the Lord. And who loses honor? Those who refuse to obey Him. In a family, the head of the household is respected, and those who fear the Lord are honored by Him. Both the rich and the poor find their greatest glory in respecting and worshiping the Lord. It is wrong to insult a wise poor person, just as it is wrong to praise someone who lives wickedly.

Princes, judges, and rulers may earn respect, but no one is greater than a person who fears the Lord. A wise servant will be honored, even among those who are free, and someone with knowledge won't complain about their situation. Don't brag about how smart you are while you work, and don't boast about your endurance during hard times. It is much better to work hard and have plenty than to be proud while struggling with hunger. My child, stay humble and only take credit for what you truly deserve.

How can you respect someone who brings harm to themselves? And how can honor be given to someone who treats their own life carelessly? A poor person can be respected for their wisdom, while a rich person is admired for their wealth. But if a poor person is honored, imagine how much greater their respect would be if they were wealthy. And if a rich person is disgraced, imagine how much worse their shame would be if they were poor.

Chapter 11

The wisdom of a humble person lifts them up and brings them into the company of important people. Don't admire someone just because they look good, and don't ignore someone just because of their appearance. Even though the bee is small compared to other flying creatures, it makes some of the sweetest honey. Don't brag about your clothes or take pride in awards, because the Lord's works are often amazing yet hidden from human eyes.

Many kings have been brought down and forced to sit on the ground, while those who were once ignored have been honored. Many powerful people have lost everything, and famous leaders have been given over to others. Don't judge anyone before you understand their situation. First, take the time to look into the matter, then offer your opinion. Don't answer before you've listened, and never interrupt someone when they are speaking. Stay away from arguments that don't involve you, and don't take sides with sinners in their disputes.

My child, don't take on too many tasks at once, or you'll end up making mistakes. If you chase after too much, you'll accomplish nothing, and avoiding problems won't guarantee you'll stay safe. Some people work endlessly but still fall behind, while others who seem weak and poor, with little strength, still manage to succeed. The Lord shows kindness to them, lifting them out of their struggles and surprising those who once looked down on them.

Both good and bad things, life and death, poverty and wealth—all come from the Lord. The blessings of the Lord remain with the righteous, and His gifts bring lasting success. Some people gain wealth through hard work and discipline, enjoying the rewards of their efforts, but in the end, they leave it all behind, never knowing how soon their time will come. Stay committed to your work, do it faithfully, and continue your efforts as you grow older.

Don't be jealous when sinners seem to succeed. Trust in the Lord and keep working hard, because God can turn a poor person into a wealthy one in an instant. His blessings can make the righteous successful overnight. Don't say, "There's nothing left for me," or, "What good can still happen to me?" Also, don't think, "I have everything I need, and nothing bad will ever happen to me." When people are happy, they forget their struggles, and when they face hardship, they forget the good times.

It's easy for the Lord to repay people for their actions when their lives come to an end. A single moment of suffering can erase years of happiness. In the end, a person's true character is revealed. Don't say someone is truly happy until their life is over, because their legacy is shown in how they are remembered and in the lives of their children.

Be careful about who you allow into your home, because some people are full of tricks and deceit. A proud person's heart is like a bird trapped in a cage, always looking for weaknesses, like a spy searching for an opportunity. They twist good things into bad and find faults even in things that deserve praise. A tiny spark can start a huge fire, and a sinful person waits for the right moment to harm others.

Stay away from those who do evil, because their schemes can ruin your reputation forever. If you let the wrong person into your home, they might create arguments and bring conflict into your family.

Chapter 12

When you choose to do good, be careful who you help so your kindness isn't wasted. Help those who live righteously, and you will be rewarded—if not by them, then by the Lord. But someone who constantly does wrong and refuses to give to others will not receive any blessings.

Give to those who do good, but don't support those who live in wickedness. Help those in need, but don't assist the ungodly. Don't give them food or resources, or they might turn against you, and later, you'll regret helping them. The Lord despises those who do evil and will bring judgment upon them. Do good to the righteous, but don't encourage the wicked.

A friend's loyalty isn't tested when life is easy, and an enemy can't stay hidden when trouble comes. When someone is successful, their enemies will resent them, and when they struggle, even their friends might leave them. Never put your trust in an enemy, because their wickedness is as persistent as rust on metal.

Even if your enemy pretends to be humble and acts like they have changed, be cautious. They may seem harmless for a while, but their true nature will show eventually. Don't let them stand beside you, or they might push you aside and take your place. Don't put them in a position of power, or they will try to take what's yours. When that happens, you'll remember this advice and regret not listening to it.

No one feels sorry for a snake charmer who gets bitten by a snake or for someone who approaches a wild animal and gets attacked. In the same way, no one will pity you if you choose to associate with a sinner and end up suffering because of it. A sinner may stay close to you for a while, but when trouble comes, they will leave without hesitation.

Your enemy might speak kindly and use flattering words, but in his heart, he is planning your downfall. He may even shed tears to seem sincere, but if given the chance, he will hurt you worse than before. When you face difficulties, he will be there—not to help you, but to take advantage of your weakness. He might act like he's offering support, but his real goal is to make you fail. He will mock you with his actions, whisper behind your back, and his true nature will be revealed in the way he looks at you and treats you.

Chapter 13

Anyone who touches tar will get sticky, and anyone who spends time with arrogant people will start acting like them. Don't take on more than you can handle, and don't try to be close to someone much stronger or richer than you. A fragile clay pot can't be friends with a sturdy metal kettle—if they collide, the clay pot will break.

A rich person can do wrong and still act tough, but a poor person, even when wronged, will have to apologize. If you are useful to a wealthy person, he will take advantage of you, but if you ever need help, he will turn his back on you. As long as you have something he wants, he'll stick around, but once he's taken all he can, he won't feel bad about leaving you empty-handed.

When he needs something from you, he'll act friendly and make you think he cares. He'll smile, pretend to be generous, and ask, "What do you need?" But behind the scenes, he's planning how to take more from you than you ever expected. Once he's done using you, he'll laugh at you, walk away without a second thought, and never feel guilty.

Be careful not to let yourself be fooled while trying to enjoy life. If a powerful person invites you somewhere, act humbly, and you may be invited back. But don't try too hard to impress him, or he'll push you away. At the same time, don't act too distant, or he might forget about you completely.

Don't assume you're on the same level as him, and don't believe everything he says. He may flatter you to see how you respond, but he's really watching you closely. A person who can't keep a secret can't be trusted. When the time is right, he won't hesitate to harm you or take advantage of you.

Keep your thoughts to yourself and be careful what you say, because you're walking on uncertain and dangerous ground.

Chapter 14

Every creature is drawn to its own kind, and people naturally connect with those who are similar to them. Each being stays with its group, and humans are no different. A wolf cannot be friends with a lamb, just as sinners and the godly cannot truly get along. A hyena and a dog don't live together peacefully, just like the rich and the poor often find themselves in conflict.

Lions hunt wild donkeys in the wilderness, and in the same way, the wealthy take advantage of the poor. A proud person looks down on those who are humble, just as a rich person often despises the poor. When a wealthy person faces trouble, they have plenty of supporters, but when a poor person struggles, even their friends turn away. If a rich person fails, many people will come to their aid and defend them, even if they are wrong. But if a poor person makes a mistake, they are criticized, and even when they speak wisely, no one listens.

When a rich person speaks, people fall silent and praise their words. But if a poor person tries to speak, others ignore them and say,

"Who is this?" If they make a small mistake, people push them down even further. Wealth is a gift when it comes without wrongdoing, but the ungodly see poverty as something shameful.

A person's heart is reflected in their face—whether they feel joy or sorrow. A cheerful face shows a happy heart, but wise thoughts require deep reflection. Blessed is the one who speaks with wisdom and avoids suffering caused by their own sins. Happy is the person whose heart is at peace and who holds onto hope.

Wealth is wasted on those who hoard it—what good is money if they never use it? A miser saves by denying themselves happiness, only for others to enjoy what they've gathered after they're gone. If someone doesn't treat themselves well, how can they be kind to others? They don't even enjoy their own possessions.

No one is more miserable than a person who refuses to enjoy life—that's their punishment for being greedy. Even when they do something good, they quickly forget it, and in the end, their selfishness is clear. A miser is harsh and turns away from those in need. Greedy people are never satisfied with what they have because their selfishness eats away at them. They even begrudge the bread on their own table.

My child, enjoy the good things you have and honor the Lord with your offerings. Remember, death comes when you least expect it. Be generous to your friends while you can, and share as much as you are able. Don't let life's pleasures pass you by or let your desires slip through your fingers. In the end, everything you worked for will belong to someone else. What you've earned will be divided among others when you're gone.

So enjoy life, give freely, and receive with gratitude, because there are no luxuries in the grave. Life is like the leaves on a tree—some fall, and others grow. Generations come and go, just like the seasons. Every effort fades, and its maker leaves with it.

Blessed is the one who reflects on wisdom and lets understanding shape their thoughts. Those who carefully seek wisdom will uncover her secrets. Chase after her like a hunter and be patient as her path unfolds. Look through her windows and listen at her doors. Stay close to her home and secure yourself to her firmly.

Make your home near her and rest in the goodness she brings. Let her shelter your children and provide shade for them under her branches. She will protect you from life's hardships and cover you with her beauty.

Chapter 15

Those who respect the Lord will follow His ways, and those who stay committed to His teachings will find wisdom. Wisdom will come to them like a caring mother and hold them close like a loving bride. She will nourish them with understanding and give them the refreshing water of wisdom to drink.

They will rely on her and remain steady. They will trust in her and never feel ashamed. Wisdom will lift them up above others and give them the confidence to speak in public. They will receive joy, honor, and a lasting reputation.

Foolish people cannot understand wisdom, and sinners cannot even recognize her. She stays far away from the arrogant, and liars quickly forget about her. Praise does not belong in the mouths of sinners, for the Lord does not allow them to have it. True praise comes from wisdom, and the Lord makes sure it continues.

Do not say, "The Lord made me do wrong," because He never leads anyone toward what He hates. Do not claim, "He caused me to sin," because the Lord has no use for those who choose evil. He despises all wickedness, and those who respect Him will turn away from it.

From the very beginning, He created people and gave them the freedom to choose their own path. If you truly want to, you can follow His commandments—it's completely up to you. He has placed fire and water before you, and you are free to choose either one.

Life and death are in front of every person, and they will receive whichever one they reach for. The Lord's wisdom is beyond understanding. He is all-powerful and sees everything. His eyes are always watching over those who honor Him, and He knows all of their actions.

The Lord has never told anyone to do evil, and He has never given permission for anyone to sin.

Chapter 16

Do not wish for many children if they will not live righteously, and do not be proud of ungodly offspring. If your children grow in number, do not rejoice unless they respect the Lord. Do not place your hopes in them simply because they are many, for one righteous child is better than a thousand, and it is better to have no children than to raise those who turn away from God.

A single wise person can restore a city, but a group of wicked people will bring it to ruin. I have seen these truths with my own eyes and heard of even greater ones. Among sinners, the fire of judgment will burn, and in nations that reject God, His wrath will be unleashed.

God did not spare the mighty giants of ancient times who became proud and rebelled. He showed no mercy to the arrogant people of Sodom, whom He despised for their pride. He did not pity those who perished in their sins, nor did He spare the six hundred thousand soldiers who hardened their hearts against Him. Even one stubborn person rarely escapes punishment, for God is both merciful and just. He forgives, but He also brings judgment.

His mercy is as great as His discipline, and He judges everyone according to their actions. A sinner will not get away with what they have taken, and the perseverance of the righteous will not be ignored. God rewards every good deed and repays everyone according to what they deserve.

Do not say, "The Lord does not see me," or, "I am just one person among many, and He will forget me." Do not think, "What does my life matter compared to all of creation?" Look at the heavens, the deep oceans, and the earth—they all tremble at His presence. The mountains shake, and the foundations of the world quake when He looks at them. No human mind can fully understand these things, for who can truly comprehend His ways?

Most of His works remain hidden, like a storm before it appears. Who can declare all His acts of righteousness or fully understand His promises that seem far off? Only a foolish and unwise person refuses to see these truths.

My child, listen to me and learn wisdom. Pay attention to my words and let them guide your heart. I will teach you carefully and provide knowledge with accuracy.

God's works were set in place from the beginning, and He established their purpose when creation began. He arranged everything for all time and determined how each generation would unfold. His creations do not grow tired or stop working, and no one can interfere with the order He has commanded. They obey His word without hesitation.

Then, the Lord looked upon the earth and blessed it richly. He filled its surface with all kinds of living creatures, and in time, they return to the earth from which they came.

Chapter 17

The Lord created humans from the earth, and one day, they will return to it. He decided how long they would live and gave them control over everything on the earth. He made them strong according to their nature and formed them in His own image. He placed fear of humans in all living creatures and gave people authority over animals and birds.

He gave humans the ability to think, speak, see, hear, and understand. He filled their minds with wisdom and taught them to recognize right from wrong. He placed His attention on their hearts and showed them the wonders of His creations.

They were made to honor His holy name and speak of His greatness. He gave them knowledge and entrusted them with His teachings as a lasting gift. He made an everlasting covenant with them and revealed His commandments. They witnessed His glory and heard the power of His voice.

He instructed them to stay away from evil and taught them how to treat one another with fairness. Their actions are always seen by Him, and nothing is hidden from His sight.

He appointed leaders over every nation, but Israel remains His chosen people.

Chapter 18

Everything people do is as clear as day to the Lord, and He always watches the paths they take. Nothing is hidden from Him, and all their sins are completely visible to Him.

The Lord values acts of kindness like a precious seal, and He treasures mercy as something incredibly important. At the right time, He will repay everyone for what they have done, returning their actions to them. But for those who turn back to Him, He offers forgiveness and brings comfort to those who feel hopeless.

Turn back to the Lord and leave your sins behind. Pray to Him and stop doing what offends Him. Return to the Most High and give up your wrongdoing. Hate what is evil. Who can praise the Lord from the grave? Only the living can give thanks. The dead cannot express gratitude, just as someone who no longer exists cannot honor Him. It is the living, those who still have breath and strength, who can glorify the Lord.

The Lord's mercy is endless, and He forgives those who repent and come back to Him. People have limits, and no one lives forever. Even the bright sun can be covered by an eclipse, and human nature often leads to mistakes. The Lord watches over everything from the heights of heaven, but to Him, people are like dust and ashes.

The eternal Lord created everything. He alone is truly righteous and just. No one can fully explain His works, nor can anyone completely understand His mighty deeds. Who can measure the power of His glory? Who can grasp the depth of His mercy? His wonders cannot be added to or taken away, and no one can fully understand them. When someone thinks they have figured it all out, they are only at the beginning. When they stop searching, they are left in awe.

What are people, and what purpose do we serve? What good do we bring, and what harm do we cause? Even at best, human life is short—just a tiny drop in the vast ocean of time or a small pebble compared to eternity. Because of this, the Lord is patient with people and pours out His mercy. He sees their struggles and increases His forgiveness toward them.

People can only show kindness to those around them, but the Lord's mercy extends to everyone. He corrects, teaches, and guides people like a shepherd leading his sheep. He is compassionate toward those who accept His discipline and choose to follow His ways.

My child, don't ruin your good deeds with harsh words or criticism when helping others. Just as dew cools the heat, a kind word is better than any gift. A kind word can be more valuable than a present, and both come naturally from a generous heart.

A foolish person is rude and ungrateful, while a stingy person gives with bitterness, leaving others feeling discouraged. Learn before you speak, and take care of your health before you get sick. Reflect on yourself before judging others, and you may find mercy when you are the one being judged. Humble yourself before trouble comes, and when you make mistakes, turn back and make things right.

Don't delay in keeping your promises, and don't wait until the end of your life to free yourself from your obligations. Think carefully before making commitments, and don't act as if you are testing the Lord. Remember that consequences can come at the end of life and that judgment may arrive when you least expect it. In good times, remember the days when you struggled. During times of success, think back to moments of hardship.

Life can change quickly—from morning to evening, everything can shift in an instant before the Lord. A wise person is careful in all things and avoids falling into sin. Those who have understanding seek wisdom and are grateful when they find it. Those who learn the meaning of wise sayings grow wiser and share meaningful words with others.

Don't give in to every desire, and keep your cravings under control. If you let your desires control you, they will make you a joke to your enemies. Avoid overindulging in luxury, and don't let it become a burden. Don't end up begging because you spent all your money on extravagant feasts and pleasures when you have nothing left.

Chapter 19

A worker who spends too much time drinking will never become rich. Someone who ignores small responsibilities will eventually lose everything. Both alcohol and unhealthy relationships can mislead even the smartest people, and anyone who wastes their time with unfaithful partners is acting foolishly. A person like that will end up with nothing but regret and shame, and their reckless lifestyle will destroy them.

Trusting others too quickly is not wise, and those who keep making bad choices only hurt themselves. Enjoying wrongdoing will lead to judgment, but avoiding gossip will help you stay out of trouble.

If you can keep a secret, people will trust you. Whether the information comes from a friend or an enemy, keep it to yourself unless staying silent would cause harm. If people find out you have spread their secrets, they may come to dislike you. If someone tells you something in confidence, respect their trust. Staying quiet takes self-control, but it won't hurt you to do so.

A fool finds it hard to keep a secret, like a woman struggling in childbirth. Gossiping is as painful to a fool as a thorn stuck deep in the skin. If you suspect your friend of wrongdoing, ask them—it's possible they didn't do it, or if they did, they might decide not to do it again. In the same way, if you think your neighbor said something harmful, talk to them about it. They may not have said it, or they may be more careful about their words in the future.

Be cautious in your friendships because gossip and slander are common. Don't believe everything you hear. People make mistakes, but often they don't mean to. Who hasn't, at some point, said something foolish? If someone wrongs you, correct them kindly before getting angry, and let God's laws guide your actions.

True wisdom begins with respecting the Lord. Following His commandments is where wisdom is found. Any knowledge that is used to do harm is not real wisdom. The ideas of those who love sin will only lead to bad decisions and disaster. Some things are truly disgraceful, and some people completely lack understanding.

It is better to know a little but have a deep respect for God than to be highly intelligent while ignoring His ways. Some people use their cleverness unfairly, twisting the truth to get what they want. Others pretend to be humble, lowering their heads and acting modestly, but inside, they are full of deceit. They may appear harmless, but if given the chance, they will take advantage of you. If they don't have the power to act on their selfish plans right away, they will wait patiently for the right moment.

A person's character can often be seen in their appearance. Someone with wisdom can often be recognized by their expression. The way a person dresses, their laughter, and even how they carry themselves say a lot about who they really are.

Chapter 20

Sometimes, it's better to stay silent than to correct someone. Giving advice calmly is more effective than reacting in anger. Admitting when you're wrong can help prevent bigger problems.

The desire of someone unable to marry for a bride is as pointless as trying to force justice through violence. Some people are respected for being quiet, while others are disliked for talking too much. Some stay silent because they have nothing important to say, while others know that silence is sometimes the best choice. A wise person speaks at the right moment, but a fool talks nonstop and misses opportunities. Talking too much can lead to resentment, and those who take power selfishly will face opposition.

Sometimes, bad luck can turn into success, while success can lead to trouble. Some gifts have no real benefit, while others bring even greater rewards. Fame can sometimes lead to downfall, while those who start with nothing may rise to greatness. Some people make small choices that lead to huge losses in the long run.

A wise person is admired for their words, but foolish jokes have no meaning. Gifts from a fool are useless because they come with expectations. A fool gives sparingly but expects endless praise, boasting about their generosity. They lend today and demand repayment tomorrow, making them difficult to be around.

A fool complains, "I have no friends, and no one appreciates my kindness. Even those who eat my food talk behind my back." People like this become the target of jokes and gossip. It is better to trip on a rock than to stumble with your words because once a fool messes up, their downfall is quick.

A story told at the wrong time by someone who lacks grace becomes a joke among those who don't understand. When a fool shares a wise saying, people ignore it because it's shared in the wrong way. Some people avoid sin, not because they are good, but because they don't have the opportunity to do wrong. They rest without worries. Others ruin their own lives with foolish decisions, breaking promises and turning friends into enemies for no reason.

A lie damages a person's reputation, and foolish people will keep repeating it. A thief is less shameful than a constant liar, but both will eventually face destruction. A liar's disgrace never goes away, and their shame follows them forever. Wise words lead to success, and those with understanding earn the respect of important people.

A hardworking farmer enjoys a good harvest, and those who earn the favor of leaders may have their mistakes overlooked. Bribes and gifts can influence even the wisest person, silencing criticism like a muzzle stops a voice.

Wisdom that is hidden, like a treasure that is never found, is useless. It's better to keep your foolishness hidden than to hide your wisdom.

Chapter 21

If you've done something wrong, my child, don't do it again. Instead, ask for forgiveness and turn away from it. Stay far from sin, just like you would avoid a poisonous snake—if you get too close, it will attack. Its bite is deadly, like a lion's, and it can destroy lives. Sin is like a sharp sword that cuts deep, leaving wounds that never fully heal.

Wealth can disappear because of fear and violence, and arrogance will lead to destruction. The prayers of the poor reach God, and He responds quickly with justice. Those who reject correction follow the path of sinners, but those who respect the Lord feel regret and change their ways.

Someone who speaks boldly may become famous, but a truly wise person recognizes their own mistakes. Building a house with stolen money is like digging your own grave. A group of wicked people is like dry straw, ready to catch fire. A sinner's path may seem easy at first, but it leads to disaster.

Those who follow God's law understand its purpose, and true wisdom starts with respecting Him. A person who lacks understanding resists learning, and even intelligence can turn into foolishness without proper guidance. Wisdom flows like a river from the heart of a wise person, and their words bring life to others.

A fool's mind is like a broken jar—it can't hold wisdom. A wise person hears good advice and values it, making it even more useful, but a careless person hears the same advice and ignores it. A fool's constant talking creates problems, while wise words bring peace.

A thoughtful person's words are treasured in conversations, and people remember what they say. But to a fool, wisdom feels like a collapsing house, and their understanding is nothing but meaningless chatter. A fool sees discipline as a punishment, something they want to escape.

A fool laughs loudly without reason, while a wise person smiles with quiet control. To the wise, learning is like a valuable piece of jewelry that makes them better. A fool rushes into a house without thinking, but an experienced person approaches carefully. A fool peeks inside without shame, while a respectful person waits patiently.

Eavesdropping is rude and disrespectful, but a wise person avoids this kind of behavior. It offends others, while the wise choose their words carefully. A fool speaks without thinking, letting their thoughts spill out, but wise people speak only after careful reflection.

When a wicked person curses someone else, the curse often comes back to them. Someone who spreads gossip brings shame on themselves and is disliked wherever they go.

Chapter 22

A lazy person is like a dirty rock that people laugh at in disgust. He is also like a pile of garbage—anyone who touches him will quickly shake him off.

A rebellious child brings shame to his father, and a foolish daughter causes him deep sadness. A wise daughter will find a good husband, but a disrespectful one brings pain to her father. A proud and arrogant daughter embarrasses both her father and husband, and they will grow to resent her.

Speaking at the wrong time is like playing cheerful music at a funeral—it doesn't fit. But correction and discipline bring wisdom in every situation. Teaching a fool is as pointless as trying to glue together broken pottery or waking someone who is deeply asleep. Trying to explain something to them is like talking to someone who is half-asleep—they'll just ask, "What are you talking about?"

Mourn for the dead because they have lost their life, but mourn even more for a fool because they lack understanding. It's better to grieve for the dead because they are at peace, while a fool's life is filled with misery. Mourning for the dead lasts seven days, but dealing with a fool or a wicked person can bring sorrow for a lifetime.

Don't waste your time talking to a fool, and don't spend too much time with those who lack sense. Stay away from them, or you'll get caught up in their troubles and foolishness. Walk away, and you'll find peace, free from their nonsense.

What is heavier than lead? Dealing with a fool. Carrying a heavy load of sand, salt, or iron is easier than dealing with someone who refuses to understand.

Wood that is tightly fastened won't come loose, and a heart that is filled with wisdom will stay steady. A strong mind full of understanding is like smooth plaster on a solid wall—it won't crumble easily.

Fences built on a hill can't stand against strong winds, just like the weak thoughts of a coward will collapse at the first sign of fear. If you poke someone in the eye, they will cry, and if you hurt someone's heart, their emotions will show. Throwing a stone at birds will make them scatter, and insulting a friend can destroy a relationship.

If you have argued with a friend, don't lose hope—peace may still be possible. If you have spoken harshly to them, don't give up—things might still be fixed unless you have insulted them, acted with pride, shared their secrets, or betrayed them. Those things will end any friendship.

Stay loyal to your friend during hard times so you can celebrate with them when things get better. Stand by them when they struggle, and you may share in their success when they rise.

Just as smoke and steam appear before a fire, insults often lead to conflict. I will never hesitate to stand up for a friend or turn away when they need my help. Even if I suffer because of my loyalty, others will learn from my example.

Who will help me control my words and give me wisdom in what I say? I need guidance to avoid making mistakes or ruining myself with careless speech.

Chapter 23

O Lord, my Father and Master of my life, don't let me follow bad advice or make mistakes that lead me to trouble. Teach me discipline and place wisdom in my heart so I don't excuse my wrongs or fail to see my own faults. If I ignore them, my sins will only grow, and I may fall, giving my enemies a reason to celebrate my downfall.

O Lord, my Father and God of my life, protect me from arrogance and pride. Keep me from selfish desires, and don't let greed or lust control me. Do not leave me to a reckless and shameless mind.

Listen, my children, to the wisdom of controlling your words. Those who guard their speech avoid falling into traps. A sinner is destroyed by their own words, and the proud are brought down by their boasting. Do not let yourself get used to swearing, and do not take the Lord's Name lightly. Just like a servant who is often beaten carries scars, a person who swears carelessly will never be free from guilt.

Someone who swears without thinking fills their life with sin, and trouble will follow them. If they sin, they are to blame. If they ignore their mistakes, they only make things worse. If they lie under oath, they won't escape judgment, and their home will suffer because of it.

There are words that bring death. Let such speech never be found among God's people. Those who follow the Lord avoid such sin. Do not let crude or offensive language become a habit, for it leads to further wrongdoing.

When you sit among wise and respected people, remember your parents and their teachings. Do not act foolishly or forget their guidance, because bad habits will embarrass you and make you regret your actions. Someone who constantly speaks harshly will never change, no matter how long they live.

There are two types of people who increase sin, and a third who invites God's anger. Lust is like a fire that destroys everything in its path. A person who is ruled by desire will never be satisfied until it ruins them.

To someone controlled by lust, every opportunity to sin seems tempting, and they will not stop until their actions lead to disaster. A man who is unfaithful to his wife thinks, "No one sees me. The darkness hides me, and the walls protect me. No one will find out. Who do I have to fear? Surely God won't remember my sins."

This man worries about being judged by people but forgets that the Lord sees everything. His eyes are brighter than the sun, watching every path and uncovering every hidden place. The Lord has seen all things since the beginning and continues to witness every action. This man will be punished in the open, and his downfall will come when he least expects it.

The same is true for a wife who leaves her husband and has children with another man. First, she disobeyed God's law. Second, she betrayed her husband. Third, she committed adultery and bore children from another man. She will face judgment before her community, and her shame will affect her family.

Her children will not prosper, her family line will fade, and she will leave no lasting legacy. Her name will serve as a warning, and her disgrace will never be forgotten. Those who witness her downfall will understand that nothing is greater than fearing the Lord and nothing is better than obeying His commandments.

Chapter 24

Wisdom speaks with pride and declares her greatness among her people. She makes her voice heard in the assembly of the Most High and reveals her glory in His presence.

"I came from the mouth of the Most High and spread across the earth like a mist. I lived in the highest places, and my throne stood in a pillar of cloud. I traveled alone through the heavens and walked through the deep waters below. I ruled over the waves of the sea, the earth, and every nation and people.

I searched for a place to rest and asked where I should settle. Then the Creator of all things gave me a command. The One who made me decided that I should dwell in Jacob and make Israel my home. He created me before time began, and I will remain forever.

I served before Him in the holy tabernacle, and He placed me in Zion. He gave me a resting place in His beloved city, and Jerusalem became my home. I took root among His chosen people, in the land given to the Lord.

I grew tall like a cedar in Lebanon and like a cypress on Mount Hermon. I flourished like a palm tree by the seashore and like the rose bushes of Jericho. I became as beautiful as an olive tree in the plains and as strong as a great tree in the city squares.

I gave off a sweet fragrance like cinnamon and balsam. My scent was like the finest myrrh, like galbanum, onycha, stacte, and frankincense in the holy tabernacle. I spread my branches like a mighty oak, showing both beauty and grace.

I blossomed like a vine, and my flowers bore rich and abundant fruit.

"Come to me, all who desire wisdom, and be filled with my fruits. My memory is sweeter than honey, and my inheritance is more delightful than the honeycomb. Those who partake of me will always want more, and those who drink of me will thirst for more. Whoever follows me will never be ashamed, and those who work with me will not fall into sin."

All of these teachings are found in the book of the covenant of the Most High, the law that Moses gave as an inheritance to the people of Jacob.

Wisdom flows like the Pishon and Tigris rivers in the early harvest. Understanding is as plentiful as the waters of the Euphrates and Jordan during the time of gathering. Instruction shines as brightly as light, like the Gihon River during the grape harvest.

No one has fully grasped wisdom at the beginning, and no one will completely understand her at the end. Her thoughts are as vast as the ocean, and her counsel is as deep as the great waters.

I flowed like a canal from a river, like an irrigation stream into a garden. I said, "I will water my plants and drench their roots." Suddenly, my stream became a river, and my river swelled into a sea.

I will continue to shine wisdom like the morning sun and make knowledge clear from afar. I will pour out teachings like prophecy and leave them for all future generations.

Understand that my work is not for myself alone but for all who truly seek wisdom."

Chapter 25

I find joy in three things that are beautiful to both God and people: family members living in harmony, neighbors treating each other with kindness, and a husband and wife supporting each other with love. But there are three types of people I can't stand, and their behavior deeply bothers me: a poor man who is arrogant, a rich man who lies, and an old man who foolishly chases after sinful desires.

If you don't save or plan wisely when you're young, how can you expect to have anything when you're old? It's a wonderful thing when older people have good judgment, and it's a blessing when elders share their wisdom and give thoughtful advice. The wisdom of older men is valuable, and the understanding of respected elders is priceless.

Their experience is like a crown of honor, and their greatest achievement is their deep respect for God.

There are nine things I have thought about, and in my heart, I see them as blessings. The tenth, I will now say out loud: a man who finds joy in his children and someone who lives to see his enemies defeated. Blessed is the man who has a wise wife, who speaks carefully and avoids careless words, and who has never been forced to serve an unworthy person. Happy is the one who makes good decisions and speaks wisely to those who listen. Wisdom is a great gift, but no one is greater than the person who deeply respects God. Respect for the Lord is the most important thing. Who can compare to someone who truly honors Him?

Nothing is harder to bear than a broken heart. No wickedness is worse than the cruelty of a bad woman. No disaster feels heavier than betrayal by those who hate you. No revenge is more painful than that of an enemy. There is no poison more dangerous than a snake's bite, and no anger worse than an enemy's rage.

I would rather live with a lion or a dragon than share a home with an evil woman. Her wickedness shows even on her face, making her expression as dark and frightening as a bear's. Her husband will sit with his neighbors, sighing in sorrow when he hears them whispering about her. There is no wickedness worse than what a bad woman can do. A woman like that is truly a punishment meant for sinners.

Living with a nagging wife is as tiring for a quiet man as climbing a steep hill is for an elderly person. Don't be fooled by a woman's beauty, and don't desire her just for her looks. If a woman takes over her husband's role as the provider, it leads to arguments, disrespect, and shame. A bad wife brings pain to her husband's heart, sadness to his face, and deep sorrow to his soul. A wife who doesn't bring joy to her husband is like weak hands or unsteady knees that cannot hold him up.

Sin entered the world through a woman, and because of that, we all face death. Don't let water spill where it shouldn't, and don't let a wicked woman say whatever she wants without control. If she refuses to listen to reason, it's better to separate from her completely.

Chapter 26

A man with a good wife is truly fortunate. His life will feel as if his days are twice as long. A loving and faithful wife brings happiness to her husband, and he will enjoy his years in peace. A good wife is a wonderful gift, given to those who respect and honor the Lord. No matter if a man is rich or poor, a kind and loving wife will always bring joy to his heart.

There are three things that make me afraid, and for the fourth, I pray: false rumors spreading through a city, a violent mob coming together, and being wrongly accused. These things are worse than death. A jealous wife brings sorrow and pain; her harsh words make her anger obvious to everyone. A wicked wife is like a heavy burden, and living with her is as risky as grabbing a scorpion. A wife who drinks too much causes shame and embarrassment, and she cannot hide her disgrace.

You can tell if a woman is unfaithful by the way she looks at others; her eyes reveal her intentions. Watch over a strong-willed daughter so she doesn't take advantage of her freedom and act recklessly. Be cautious of an inappropriate glance, and don't be surprised if it leads to trouble. She will be like a thirsty traveler drinking from any stream she finds. She will sit on every street corner, accepting anyone without restraint.

A good wife brings happiness to her husband, and her wisdom makes him stronger. A quiet and gentle woman is a gift from the Lord, and nothing is as valuable as a well-guided heart. A modest wife is a blessing beyond measure; her self-control is worth more than any treasure. The beauty of a good wife shines in her well-kept home, like the sunrise in the sky. Just as a beautiful face looks best on a balanced body, a graceful and faithful woman is like a lamp that brightens a sacred space. A woman with steady feet and a strong heart is like golden pillars set on a silver base.

There are two things that deeply trouble me, and a third that fills me with anger: a warrior who struggles with poverty, wise men who are treated as worthless, and someone who abandons righteousness to return to sin. The Lord will prepare such a person for judgment. It is hard for a merchant to stay completely honest, and a shopkeeper must work hard to avoid sin.

Chapter 27

Many people make bad choices when they are obsessed with getting rich. Someone desperate for wealth often ignores what is right and wrong. Just as a nail holds two stones together, sin is often mixed into business dealings. Without a strong foundation in respect for the Lord, a household will quickly fall apart.

When you shake a sieve, the unwanted bits are left behind. In the same way, a person's weaknesses are revealed through their thoughts. A potter tests his pottery in fire, and a person's true nature is shown by what's in their heart. Just like a tree's health is known by its fruit, a person's words reveal the condition of their soul. Don't be too quick to praise someone—listen to their thoughts first. Their words will show you who they really are.

If you seek righteousness, you will find it, and it will become part of you like a beautiful robe. Birds stay with their own kind, and truth gathers around those who live by it. Just as a lion waits to attack its prey, sin lies in wait for those who wander from the right path.

A wise person speaks carefully, but a fool is as unpredictable as the changing moon. Stay away from people who lack understanding and instead surround yourself with thoughtful, wise individuals. The way fools talk is offensive; their laughter is wild and full of sin. Their loud, disrespectful words make others avoid them, and their constant arguing frustrates those around them. Proud people start fights that can quickly turn violent, and their insults can deeply wound others.

Someone who can't keep a secret will ruin friendships and never gain trust. Stay loyal to your friends and protect their private matters. If you betray them, you might as well be an enemy. Losing a friend is like letting a bird fly out of your hand—you won't be able to catch it again. Don't chase after them; they'll be as impossible to reach as a deer running from danger.

Wounds can heal, and arguments can be solved, but revealing someone's secrets causes lasting damage. A person who winks while talking is usually up to no good, and those who notice it will stay away from them. They may say nice things to your face, but later, they twist your words and use them against you. I dislike many things, but this kind of behavior is the worst—and God hates it too.

Anyone who throws a stone straight up will have it fall back on their own head. A person who attacks others unfairly will end up getting hurt. Those who dig a pit to trap someone will fall into it themselves. Evil always finds its way back to the person who does it, often when they least expect it.

Proud people use insults and mockery to hurt others, but judgment is waiting for them like a lion ready to attack. Those who enjoy watching good people fail will end up trapped by their own schemes. Their lives will be filled with misery before they come to an end. Anger and hatred destroy people, and only those who refuse to change will hold on to them.

Chapter 28

Those who seek revenge will face God's judgment, and He will hold them accountable for their own sins. If you forgive others for their mistakes, God will forgive you when you ask for mercy. How can someone hold a grudge and still expect the Lord to heal them? If a person refuses to show kindness to others, how can they expect kindness for themselves?

If you cling to anger, who will stand up for you when you need forgiveness? Think about how short life is and let go of hate. Remember that one day, everyone returns to dust, so stay focused on following God's commands. Keep His teachings in your heart and don't hold grudges. Instead, remember the agreement made with the Most High and forgive those who acted out of ignorance.

Avoid conflict, and you will avoid sin. An angry person creates division, and a troublemaker ruins friendships and peace between neighbors. Just as a fire grows when fed with wood, an argument grows when fueled by strong emotions. The greater the anger, the bigger the damage. A person's temper often matches their power, and their wealth can make them even more aggressive.

Jumping into an argument is like lighting a match—it can quickly turn into a disaster. If you blow on a spark, it will grow into flames, but if you spit on it, it will go out. The choice is yours. Curse those who spread gossip and lies because they have ruined the lives of many.

Lies and slander have forced people to flee their homes, destroyed cities, and brought down leaders. They have driven strong women away from what they worked hard to earn. Those who believe gossip will never have peace or live a quiet life.

A whip leaves marks on the body, but hurtful words can break a person's spirit. While many have died from weapons, even more have been destroyed by cruel words. Blessed are those who have never suffered because of slander, who have never carried its burden or felt its weight.

Slander is heavier than iron and stronger than chains. Its impact can feel worse than death itself. But those who live righteously will not be overcome by it. It cannot burn them or bring them down. However, those who turn away from God will be destroyed by it. Gossip and lies will devour them like a roaring lion or a wild leopard ready to tear them apart.

Just as you carefully guard your valuables, you should also guard your words. Lock your mouth like a door with a strong key. Be careful what you say, or you may fall into the hands of those waiting to use your words against you.

Chapter 29

Those who are kind and generous will help their neighbors, and those who give with their own hands are following God's commands. If your neighbor is struggling, offer them a loan, and if you borrow, make sure to pay it back on time. Be honest and dependable, and you'll always find help when you need it.

Many people borrow money as if it's a gift and end up causing trouble for those who trusted them. At first, they may act humble and say nice things to win favor. But when it's time to repay, they stall, make excuses, and complain about their bad luck. If they manage to avoid paying back, the lender might be lucky to recover even a small part of what was owed. In worse cases, the borrower takes the money and turns against the lender, showing no gratitude and even responding with insults or accusations.

Because of this, many people stop lending altogether. But don't let this stop you from helping someone in need, and don't make a struggling person wait for help. Give freely when you can and don't send someone away empty-handed. Be willing to take risks to help a friend or a family member. Don't let your money sit idle, going to waste like a stone left unused. Use what you have in ways that honor God's commands, and it will be more valuable than gold. Kindness and generosity are treasures that will protect you in times of trouble. They are stronger than any shield or weapon when it comes to defending you from harm.

A generous person will stand by a neighbor's loan, but someone who lacks integrity will fail to keep their promises. If someone has risked their own money to help you, don't forget their kindness. They may have put everything on the line for your sake. But a careless person will waste the resources of someone who supported them, and an ungrateful person will turn their back on the one who rescued them.

Guaranteeing someone else's loan has ruined many successful people, tossing them around like waves in the sea. Some have lost their homes and been forced to live in foreign lands. A reckless person who makes promises without thinking will end up trapped in legal troubles. Help your neighbor as much as you can, but don't put yourself in danger while doing so.

The basics of life are simple: water, food, clothing, and a home where you can have privacy. It's better to live humbly in a small home of your own than to enjoy luxury while staying as a guest in someone else's house. Whether you have a little or a lot, learn to be content.

Moving from place to place is exhausting, especially when you're a guest who doesn't have freedom or comfort.

You might serve food and drinks to your hosts and receive no gratitude in return. Instead, they might speak to you harshly: "Come here, traveler, and serve me." Or worse, they might say, "It's time for you to leave. Someone important is coming. My family is staying over, and I need my space back."

These situations are hard for an understanding person to bear—being scolded for needing a place to stay and suffering the harsh words of those who demand repayment.

Chapter 30

A loving father corrects his child often, making sure he grows up to bring joy. A parent who teaches and disciplines his son will feel proud and gain respect from others. Raising a child well can even make his enemies jealous, and he will feel honored among his friends. Even after the father is gone, it will feel like he still lives on through his son, who reflects his values. While the father is alive, his child brings him happiness, and when he dies, he has no regrets, knowing his son will be strong and kind.

But a parent who spoils their child will always have to deal with the problems that follow, and it will hurt every time the child's bad choices bring trouble. Just like an untrained horse becomes wild, a child without discipline will grow rebellious. If you give a child too much freedom, they will make you worry. If you treat them too casually, they will cause you sadness. Don't joke around too much with them, or you might regret it later. Don't let them do whatever they want when they are young, and don't ignore foolish behavior.

Correct them while they are still young, and guide them with a firm hand. If you don't, they may become disrespectful and bring you shame. Teach them responsibility so they don't grow up without a sense of honor.

A poor man who is strong and healthy is better off than a rich man suffering from illness. Good health and a strong body are more valuable than gold and wealth. There is no treasure greater than being healthy and no joy better than having peace of mind. It is better to die than to live in constant misery, and resting in peace is better than struggling through endless sickness.

Giving gifts to someone who cannot enjoy them is pointless, like offering food to a grave. What is the use of an offering to an idol? It cannot eat or smell. In the same way, those suffering under the Lord's punishment groan in pain, unable to act—like a man longing for a wife but unable to fulfill his desire.

Don't let sadness take over your life, and don't make yourself suffer for no reason. A happy heart gives energy and makes life better, and a cheerful spirit can even help you live longer. Take care of yourself and find peace in your heart. Push sorrow away because it has ruined many lives and does nothing good. Jealousy and anger will shorten your life, and constant stress will make you age faster. Those who are happy and content will enjoy their meals and gain strength from them.

Chapter 31

Constantly worrying about money wears a person down, and stressing over wealth takes away peace of mind. Sleepless nights leave people longing for rest, but even sleep can be disturbed by sickness or anxiety. A rich person works hard to build his fortune, and when he rests, he enjoys the comforts of his wealth. A poor person works just as hard but still struggles, and even when he rests, his hunger remains.

Those who are obsessed with money will always feel guilty, and those who chase after greed will eventually be destroyed by it. Many have ruined their lives by craving riches, bringing disaster upon themselves. Greed is a trap that catches anyone who falls for its temptation. But blessed is the person who stays honest, even when they are wealthy, and does not let greed control their heart.

Who among the rich can truly be called blessed? It is the one who has used his wealth to do good for others. Who has been tested by riches but stayed honest? That person can be proud of his actions. Who had the chance to do wrong but chose to walk away, or could have hurt others but refused? That person will find lasting success and be respected by his community.

If you are invited to a big feast, don't let greed take over. Don't think, "Look at all this food!" Remember, greed is dangerous, and nothing is greedier than the eyes—they are never satisfied and always want more. Don't grab at every dish or reach for whatever looks good. Be considerate of others and show self-control.

Eat a modest amount and don't overindulge, or people might dislike your behavior. Stop eating before you are completely full as a sign of respect. Don't be greedy, or you may embarrass yourself. When eating with others, don't rush to take food before everyone else. A well-mannered person is happy with a small portion and sleeps peacefully. Eating in moderation leads to restful sleep and a clear mind the next morning. But overeating causes discomfort, sleepless nights, and regret.

If you've eaten too much, get up and take a walk—it will help you feel better. Listen to this advice, my child, and don't ignore it. In time, you will see how wise it is. Be thoughtful and disciplined in everything you do, and you'll avoid unnecessary illness. A generous host earns praise, and their kindness is remembered. But a stingy person earns criticism, and their selfishness will not be forgotten.

Don't try to impress others by drinking too much alcohol—it has ruined many lives. Just as fire tests the strength of metal, wine reveals the true character of a proud person in an argument. Wine, when enjoyed in moderation, can bring happiness. What joy is there for someone who never drinks it? It was made to lighten the heart and lift the spirit. But drinking too much leads to bitterness, anger, and fights. Drunkenness turns a fool into his worst self, weakening his body, draining his energy, and leaving him with regret.

At a gathering where wine is served, don't judge your neighbor for drinking or try to embarrass him. Avoid harsh words or demands that might ruin his mood or take away from the joy of the celebration.

Chapter 32

If you are chosen to host a feast, don't let it make you feel more important than others. Treat everyone kindly and make sure your guests are comfortable before you sit down to eat. Once you've taken care of everything, relax and enjoy the company of those around you. Your efforts will be noticed and appreciated.

If you are older, you have the right to speak, but do so wisely. Don't interrupt the music or talk over it. Don't try to show off your knowledge at the wrong time. Music at a feast is like a precious jewel in a golden setting—it adds beauty and value. A pleasant song paired with good wine is like an elegant decoration made of gold and emeralds.

If you are younger and asked to speak, keep your words short and meaningful. Speak only when invited, and don't go on for too long. Act with understanding and know when to stay quiet. If you are with important people, don't try to act like their equal or talk over others.

Just as lightning comes before thunder, respect comes to those who are humble. When the time is right, leave the gathering early instead of overstaying your welcome. Go straight home and enjoy your time there, but don't let pride lead you into wrongdoing. In all things, give thanks to your Creator, who gives you the blessings you enjoy.

Those who respect the Lord will accept correction, and those who seek Him will receive His kindness. Those who follow His law will find peace, but hypocrites will struggle with it. Those who honor the Lord will gain wisdom and shine with goodness.

A sinful person refuses to be corrected and only listens to what benefits them. A wise person values good advice, but a proud person will act foolishly, refusing to admit mistakes or learn from them. Don't act without thinking, and once you make a choice, don't constantly regret it.

Avoid paths that lead to trouble, and don't take risks that aren't necessary. Even when things seem easy, don't become careless—always stay aware. Pay attention to those around you, even your own children. In everything you do, take care of your soul, for this is the key to following the Lord's commands. Those who respect the law will listen to its teachings, and those who trust in the Lord will not be misled.

Chapter 33

No harm will come to those who respect the Lord because even in tough times, He will rescue them again and again. A wise person follows the law, but a hypocrite is as unreliable as a ship caught in a storm. Those who truly understand put their trust in the law, which guides them like a faithful messenger.

Choose your words wisely, and people will listen. Think before you speak, and give thoughtful answers. A fool's mind is restless, like a wheel that spins out of control. His thoughts are as unstable as a cart rolling unevenly. A wild horse is like an undisciplined friend, resisting anyone who tries to guide him.

Why is one day different from another when the same sun shines on all? The Lord, in His wisdom, has set certain days apart. He created seasons and special festivals, making some days sacred while others remain ordinary. All people come from the earth, just like Adam, who was made from dust. The Lord, in His wisdom, made people different and set their paths apart. Some He blessed, raising them to greatness, while others He humbled and brought down.

Just as a potter shapes clay, so the Creator molds people according to His plan. He decides their purpose and judges them as He sees fit. Good and evil oppose each other, just as life and death do. In the same way, sinners stand against the godly. Everything in creation has a balance—each thing has its opposite.

I felt like someone picking up leftover grapes after the harvesters had finished, but the Lord blessed me. My winepress was filled as if I had gathered the grapes myself. Remember, my work was not just for my own benefit but for all who seek wisdom and guidance.

Listen to me, leaders and those who guide others. Do not give control over your life to your son, wife, brother, or friend while you are still alive. Do not hand over your belongings to someone else, or you may regret it later and find yourself asking for them back. As long as you live and have strength, keep control of your life. It is better for your children to depend on you than for you to rely on them. Strive for excellence in all you do, and protect your reputation. When your time comes, distribute your inheritance, but wait until your final days to do so.

Donkeys need food, whips, and burdens, and servants need bread, discipline, and work. Keep your servant busy, and you will have peace. If you leave him idle, he may start thinking about freedom. A yoke and whip keep a servant humble, and strict discipline is needed for those who are disobedient. Keep him occupied, or idleness will lead him to trouble. Give him tasks that suit him, and if he refuses to obey, enforce stricter discipline.

Do not be cruel or unfair to anyone. If you have a servant, treat him with respect because his life was paid for with blood. Value your servant as you value yourself because you depend on him as much as he depends on you. If you mistreat him and he decides to leave, where will you go to find him?

Chapter 34

Empty hopes belong to those who lack understanding, and foolish people are misled by dreams. Chasing dreams is like trying to catch a shadow or follow the wind. Dreams are nothing more than reflections, like one face mirroring another. How can something pure come from what is impure? How can truth come from lies?

Fortune-telling, omens, and dreams are worthless. The mind is filled with illusions, just like the pain of a woman in labor. Unless a dream comes as a message from the Most High, do not trust it. Many have been deceived by dreams, failing because they relied on them too much.

Without lies, the law is fulfilled, and wisdom is found in the words of those who are faithful. A well-taught person understands much, and someone with experience speaks with wisdom. A person with little experience knows little, but those who travel and see the world gain knowledge and perspective. I have witnessed many things on my journeys, and my understanding goes deeper than words can explain.

I have faced danger, even the threat of death, but my experiences have guided and protected me.

Those who respect the Lord will thrive because they put their hope in the One who saves them. Whoever fears the Lord will not be weak or afraid, for the Lord is their strength. Blessed is the person who trusts in the Lord. Whose voice does he listen to? Who is his support? The Lord watches over those who love Him. He is their strong protector and steady foundation, their shelter from the heat, their shade at midday, their guide when they stumble, and their help in times of trouble. He lifts their spirits, brightens their eyes, and grants them health, life, and blessings.

Someone who offers a sacrifice from stolen goods disrespects the very act of giving. The sacrifices of wicked people are worthless. The Most High is not pleased with offerings from the ungodly, and no amount of gifts can make up for their sins. It is like killing a child in front of their father while pretending to make an offering. The food of the poor is their life, and taking it from them is like committing murder. Robbing someone of their means to live is like taking their life. Holding back a worker's wages is no different from shedding blood.

If one person builds something and another tears it down, what have they gained but wasted effort? If one prays while another curses, whose prayer will the Lord listen to? A person who washes after touching a dead body but then touches it again has gained nothing from washing. In the same way, someone who fasts for their sins but keeps returning to them gains nothing from fasting. Who will listen to their prayers? What good is their false humility?

Chapter 35

Whoever follows the law is like someone making many offerings, and whoever obeys the commandments gives a gift of peace. Being kind is like offering the finest flour, and helping others is like giving a thank-you offering. Turning away from evil pleases the Lord, and leaving behind sin is like making a sacrifice to make up for past mistakes. Don't come to the Lord empty-handed.

These things should be done because they are His commands. The offerings of good people bring honor to the altar, and their pleasing scent rises up to the Most High. God accepts the sacrifices of those who do what is right, and He will never forget them. Show respect for the Lord by being generous, and don't hold back when giving the first portion of what you earn. When you give, do it with a happy heart, and offer your tithe with joy.

Give to the Most High according to how much He has blessed you. Be as generous as you are able. The Lord rewards kindness, and He will repay you many times over. But don't think you can buy God's favor with gifts—He will not accept them. Don't offer anything gained dishonestly, because the Lord is a fair judge who treats everyone equally.

God does not take sides against the poor, and He listens to the prayers of those who have been wronged. He does not ignore orphans or widows when they cry out for help. Aren't a widow's tears visible on her face? Isn't her sorrow directed at the one who caused her pain?

The person who faithfully serves God will be accepted, and their prayers will reach heaven. The prayers of humble people rise like smoke through the clouds. Their prayers won't stop until they reach the Lord. They keep calling out until the Most High steps in, judges fairly, and brings justice.

The Lord will not wait forever or stay silent without limit. He will break the power of the cruel and bring justice to the nations. He will humble the proud and take away the strength of the wicked. He will repay everyone according to their actions and give them what they deserve based on their choices. He will stand up for His people and bring them joy through His mercy.

Mercy is as valuable in hard times as rain is during a drought.

Chapter 36

Have mercy on us, Lord, the God of all, and show us your kindness. Let the whole world see your power. Show your strength against the nations so they will recognize your might. Just as you revealed your holiness to us, let them now see your greatness through us. Let them understand, as we have come to know, that you alone are God—there is no other.

Show new signs and perform great wonders. Display your power and strengthen your mighty hand. Let your anger rise, and pour out your judgment. Defeat those who oppose you and bring an end to your enemies. Speed up the time you have planned and remember your promises, so that everyone may witness your mighty works. Let those who survive be consumed by fire, and may those who harm your people face their downfall. Crush the rulers of your enemies, those who boast, "We are the only ones who matter."

Bring together all the tribes of Jacob and restore them as your chosen people, just as you did before. Lord, show kindness to those who carry your name, to Israel, your firstborn. Have mercy on the city of your holy temple, Jerusalem, the place where you dwell. Fill Zion with your majesty, and let your words of truth be honored. Let your people be surrounded by your glory.

Keep the promises you made to those you created from the beginning. Fulfill the prophecies spoken in your name. Reward those who patiently wait for you so that people will trust in your prophets. Lord, listen to the prayers of your servants, just as you gave Aaron the blessing for your people. Let the whole earth know that you are the Lord, the eternal God.

The stomach can handle any food, but some meals taste better than others. The mouth enjoys fresh meat, just as a wise heart can recognize deceitful words. A stubborn heart leads to trouble, but an experienced person knows how to respond wisely.

A woman may accept any man, but some daughters are still better than others. A woman's beauty brightens her face, and nothing is more attractive to a man. If she speaks with kindness and humility, her husband will be admired. A man who finds a good wife has found a priceless treasure—a partner and a source of strength.

Without a fence, a field is open to anyone. In the same way, a man without a wife feels lonely and incomplete. Who would trust a thief who moves from city to city? In the same way, who would rely on a man with no home, who sleeps wherever he can find shelter?

Chapter 37

Everyone will say, "I'm your friend," but some people are only friends in name. Isn't it painful, even unbearable, when someone you trusted turns against you? Deceitful thoughts fill the world with lies—why do they exist?

Some friends celebrate with you when things are good but disappear when trouble comes. Others stay around only for their own gain, but when danger appears, they leave to save themselves. Never forget a true friend, and don't ignore them when life is going well for you.

Every advisor believes their advice is the best, but some only give advice that benefits themselves. Be careful when listening to others, and try to understand their true intentions. They may be looking out for their own interests and waiting to see what happens to you. Don't trust advice from someone who doesn't have faith in you, and don't share your plans with someone who envies you.

Don't ask a woman about her rival, a coward about war, a merchant about business, a buyer about selling, a jealous person about gratitude, a cruel person about kindness, a lazy person about hard work, a servant about completing a job, or an idle worker about serious business. These people won't give trustworthy advice.

Instead, seek advice from someone who follows God's ways, obeys His commandments, and cares about you as much as they care about themselves. Find someone who will stand by you even if you fail. Trust your own judgment as well, because no one knows you better than yourself. Sometimes, your own thoughts can guide you better than a group of watchmen standing guard. But above all, ask God to lead you in truth.

Use reason to make decisions, and think carefully before taking action. Four things test a person's heart: good and evil, life and death. The words we speak hold the power to shape all of them.

Some people teach many but fail to improve themselves. Others are skilled with words but are disliked and end up with nothing. They lack God's favor and miss out on wisdom. But a person who grows wise for their own soul speaks with understanding and earns trust. A wise person teaches others, and their words are dependable. They will receive many blessings, and people will call them fortunate.

A person's life is measured in days, but the days of Israel are countless. A wise person earns the trust of their community, and their name is remembered forever.

My child, reflect on your life and choices. Pay attention to what harms you and avoid it. Not everything is good for everyone, and people have different preferences. Don't overindulge in luxury, and don't be greedy with food. Eating too much can make you sick, and greed brings discomfort. Many have suffered because of their lack of self-control, but those who are mindful live longer.

Chapter 38

Respect doctors when you need their help,
    because their skill is a gift from God.
Healing comes from the Lord,
    and even kings rely on doctors.
A doctor's knowledge earns them respect,
    and they are admired by those in power.

God created medicines from the earth,
    and wise people understand their importance.
Didn't He make bitter water sweet with a piece of wood,
    showing His power through it?
He gave people knowledge
    so His wonders could be recognized.
With this knowledge, He heals the sick
    and eases the pain of those who suffer.
Pharmacists use this wisdom to prepare medicines,
    and through God's work, peace is brought to the world.

My child, when you feel sick, don't ignore it.
Pray to God, and He will help you heal.
Turn away from wrongdoing,
    and live a good life.
Cleanse your heart of sin.

Offer the best you can as a sacrifice,
    and pour oil on it according to your means.
Then, let the doctor do their job,
    for they too are part of God's creation.
Don't refuse their help,
    because their care might be what you need.
There are times when recovery depends on their skills.
Even doctors pray to God,
    asking for guidance to heal their patients
    and bring life back to them.

But remember, those who offend their Creator
    may find themselves in need of a doctor.

My child, cry for those who have passed away.
    Mourn them deeply, and show your grief.
Prepare their body with care,
    and don't neglect their burial.
Weep from your heart and express your sorrow.
Let your mourning reflect your love for them,
    but don't let it last too long—one or two days—
    so people don't criticize you.
Then, move forward and find comfort in your heart.
Too much grief can weigh you down.
A heavy heart drains your strength.

Grief lingers in difficult times,
    and life is even harder for the poor.
Don't let sadness take over your life.
Let go of sorrow,
    knowing that death is a natural part of life.
You can't bring someone back once they are gone.

Endless mourning won't help the dead,
    but it will only hurt you.
Think about how life ends,
    because your time will come too.
Yesterday it was them; tomorrow it could be you.
When the dead find peace, let their memory rest as well.
Find comfort as their spirit moves on.

Wisdom comes to those who have time to learn.
People who are free from heavy labor
    have more time to gain understanding.
But how can someone grow in wisdom
    if they spend their days plowing fields,
    finding joy in their oxen,
    and only talking about livestock?
They focus on making straight rows,
    and their minds are on tending animals.

The same goes for craftsmen and skilled workers.
They labor tirelessly, day and night.
The engraver carefully carves intricate designs,
    putting his heart into making beautiful pieces.
The blacksmith hammers hot metal,
    shaping iron into useful tools.
The fire burns his skin,
    and the sound of pounding fills his ears.
But his eyes stay locked on his creation,
    determined to make it perfect.

The potter, working at his wheel,
    is completely focused on his craft.

He shapes and molds clay with skilled hands,
    creating many useful items.
He carefully applies glaze
    and fires his pottery to perfection.

All of these workers depend on their abilities,
    and each one is skilled in their trade.
Without them, no city could function.
People wouldn't have homes or roads to walk on.

But they are not found in places of power.
They don't lead assemblies or interpret laws.
They don't teach wisdom or tell parables.
Even so, their work keeps the world running.
Their prayers are expressed through their skillful hands.

Chapter 39

Whoever is dedicated to following the law of the Most High and thinks deeply about it will search for wisdom from the past and study the words of the prophets. They will value the teachings of wise people and seek to understand the hidden meanings in parables. They will learn the deeper lessons behind proverbs and uncover the messages within riddles.

Such a person will stand among great leaders and serve in the presence of rulers. They will travel to different places, learning to distinguish between good and bad in people. Their heart will always turn toward the Lord, their Creator, and they will pray to the Most High, asking for mercy and forgiveness for their mistakes.

If it is God's will, they will be filled with wisdom and understanding. They will speak with insight and offer prayers of gratitude. They will guide others with their knowledge and reflect on the mysteries of God. They will teach the lessons they have learned and take joy in following God's law. Many will respect their wisdom, and their teachings will not be forgotten. Their name will be remembered for generations, and people from different nations will recognize their wisdom. The community of believers will honor them and speak of their knowledge.

If they stay true to their purpose, their reputation will grow beyond even the most successful people. Even after their life ends, their legacy will remain. I have much more to say, for my thoughts are as full as the bright moon. Listen to me, my children, and grow like a rose planted by a flowing stream. Let your fragrance spread like incense, bloom like a lily, and fill the air with a pleasant scent. Sing songs of praise and thank the Lord for His wonderful works.

Lift up His name and raise your voices in gratitude. Praise Him with music and joyful singing, and declare these words of thanks:

"The Lord's works are amazing, and every command is fulfilled at the right time. No one can ask, 'Why is this happening?' or 'Why is that needed?' because in His perfect timing, everything becomes clear. By His word, the waters gathered in one place, and by His command, the reservoirs were formed. His power makes all things happen, and nothing can stop His salvation.

"Everything people do is visible to Him; nothing is hidden from His sight. From eternity to eternity, He sees all things, and His wisdom covers everything. No one can question, 'Why is this so?' or 'Why is that needed?' because everything serves a purpose. His blessings flow like rivers, pouring over the earth like a flood. Just as He made the sea salty, He has reserved His judgment for those who do evil.

"His ways are clear to those who are faithful, but they are stumbling blocks for those who reject Him. From the beginning, good things were made for those who do right, while destruction was set aside for those who choose sin. The necessities of life—water, fire, iron, salt, flour, honey, milk, wine, oil, and clothing—were created for everyone's benefit. For the godly, these are blessings, but for those who turn away from God, these things can bring harm.

"The winds were made to carry out His justice, and in their fury, they bring punishment. On the day of judgment, they will act with full force to carry out the will of their Creator. Fire, hail, famine, and death—all were created as instruments of His justice. Wild animals, scorpions, snakes, and the sword exist to punish the wicked. They stand ready to obey His commands and will act when the time comes. They never fail to carry out His will."

This is what I have learned from the beginning, and I have carefully written it down after much thought: Everything the Lord does is good, and He provides what is needed at the right time. No one can say, "This is better than that," because everything is perfect when used as He intended.

So now, with all your heart and voice, sing praises and bless the name of the Lord!

Chapter 40

Life is a heavy burden that everyone must carry, passed down from the first human to every person born after. From the moment a baby is born until they return to the earth, life is full of struggles. People worry about what will happen next and fear the certainty of death.

It doesn't matter if someone is a king sitting on a throne or a poor person covered in dirt, if they wear royal robes or simple rags—everyone feels anger, jealousy, anxiety, and the fear of death. Their troubles never leave them, filling their days with stress and their nights with restless thoughts. Even in bed, sleep does not bring peace. Their dreams are filled with fears, like someone standing guard in the dark, afraid of what might come. Their heart pounds as if they are running from battle, only to wake up and realize their fears were for nothing.

Death, violence, arguments, war, disasters, hunger, suffering, and disease affect every living creature—both humans and animals—but sinners feel their weight even more. These evils exist because of the wicked, and they were the reason for the great flood. Everything that comes from the earth will return to it, just as everything that comes from water will return to the sea.

Corruption and injustice will not last forever, but faithfulness will never disappear. The riches of the wicked will dry up like a river during a drought, and their success will vanish like the sound of thunder after a storm. Generous people find joy in giving, but those who live without morals will eventually fall. The children of the wicked will not flourish, like weak roots struggling to grow on dry ground. Just as reeds by the water are pulled up before other plants, the ungodly will not stand strong for long.

Acts of kindness are like a garden full of blessings, and generosity creates a legacy that will never fade. A hardworking and content person enjoys their life, but discovering a hidden treasure is even better. Children and building a city bring honor, but a good and faithful spouse is more valuable than either. Music and wine bring joy to the heart, but the love of wisdom is even greater. A flute and a harp make beautiful sounds, but a kind and gentle voice is even sweeter.

The eye is drawn to beauty and grace, but nothing is more valuable than a field full of ripe crops. A friend or companion brings happiness, but the love between a husband and wife is even stronger. Relatives and helpers are useful in times of trouble, but giving to those in need is the best protection of all. Gold and silver can bring stability, but good advice is worth even more. Wealth and strength may lift a person's confidence, but having deep respect for the Lord is more important than both. The fear of the Lord fulfills every need, and those who have it will never go without. It is like a garden full of blessings and gives more honor than anything else.

My child, do not live by begging from others. It is better to die than to rely on people for everything. A person who depends on others for food can never truly live freely. Taking what belongs to someone else brings shame, but a wise and disciplined person avoids this disgrace. For those who lack self-respect, begging may feel easy at first, but it leads to deep humiliation and never-ending hunger.

Chapter 41

Oh, death, how hard it is to think about you for someone who is happy, with no troubles to worry about, enjoying success, good health, and all the pleasures of life. But for the poor and weak, for the elderly who are exhausted and have endured many hardships, death comes as a relief.

Don't be afraid when death calls. Think of all the people who lived before you and those who will come after. This is the path the Lord has set for every living thing. Why fight it when it is part of His plan? Whether someone lives ten years, a hundred, or even a thousand, no one can question the judgment that comes after life.

The children of wicked people often live in disgrace and among those who do evil. Their legacy fades away, and their descendants bear the shame of their actions forever. Children will blame a sinful parent because they suffer the consequences of their wrongdoing. How terrible it is for those who reject the law of the Most High! If they are born, they live under a curse, and when they die, the curse follows them. Everything that comes from the earth returns to the earth, and the wicked will pass from one misery to another.

People mourn over the bodies of the dead, but the wicked will be forgotten. Guard your reputation, for it is more valuable than gold or silver. A good life has an end, but a good name lasts forever.

My children, seek wisdom with an open and calm heart. But what good is wisdom if it is hidden, or wealth if it is never used? A fool who stays silent about his ignorance is better than a wise person who refuses to share knowledge. Pay attention to my words, for not every kind of shame is worth keeping, and not every action is honorable.

Be ashamed of doing wrong in front of your parents, of lying to a leader or someone in authority, of committing crimes before a judge or in public, of betraying a friend or partner, and of stealing while being a guest in someone's home. Be ashamed of dishonoring God's truth and breaking His covenant, of bad manners at the dinner table, or of being rude when giving or receiving gifts. Be ashamed of ignoring someone's greeting, staring at a prostitute, neglecting a relative in need, or taking back something you already gave. Do not look at another man's wife or interfere with his servant—stay far away from his home.

Do not be rude to your friends, and after giving a gift, do not humiliate the person who received it. Avoid gossip and revealing secrets. Only feel shame for things that are truly disgraceful, and you will earn the respect and admiration of others.

Chapter 42

Do not be ashamed of these things, and never commit a sin just to protect your reputation: respecting the law of the Most High and keeping His covenant, ensuring justice even when judging the guilty, settling financial matters fairly with a business partner or fellow traveler, accepting what is rightfully yours from a friend's inheritance, using honest scales and weights in all transactions, being fair in your dealings with merchants, correcting your children regularly, and disciplining a disobedient servant when necessary.

If your wife is untrustworthy, keeping important things secured is wise. When many hands are involved, make sure to safeguard your belongings. Always count and measure carefully when giving or receiving something, and keep a written record of all exchanges.

Don't be afraid to teach those who lack knowledge, even if they are older or disagree with younger people. Helping others learn will increase your own wisdom and earn you respect. A daughter can cause endless worry for her father, making him anxious at every stage of her life. When she is young, he fears she may never marry. If she does, he worries that her husband will mistreat her. While she is still at home, he fears she might make mistakes or become pregnant. If she marries, he hopes she will be faithful and have children, but he constantly worries about her future.

Keep a close watch on a rebellious daughter, or she could bring shame to your name and damage your reputation. She might become the subject of gossip, making people talk badly about you in public. Do not let yourself be distracted by every attractive person, and don't spend too much time in the company of women. Just as moths destroy clothing, a woman's bad influence can spread quickly to others.

It is better to deal with a man's wickedness than to experience the so-called kindness of a woman who brings shame and dishonor. Now I will speak about the works of the Lord and share what I have learned. His creations are revealed through His word. The sun shines brightly, watching over everything, and all His works are filled with His glory.

No one can fully understand all of God's amazing works. He has carefully designed everything, filling the world with beauty and order. He knows the deepest parts of the earth and the hidden thoughts in every heart. Nothing is a mystery to Him because the Most High sees and understands all things. He knows the signs of the world, reveals the past, predicts the future, and uncovers what is hidden.

No thought is hidden from Him, and no word escapes His notice. With His wisdom, He controls everything. He is eternal, with no beginning or end. Nothing can be added to His creation, and nothing has been taken away. He needs no help or guidance.

His works are beyond imagination! Even the smallest detail of creation reflects His greatness. Everything He has made will last forever and serves its purpose according to His plan. All things follow His commands. Everything exists in pairs, balancing and complementing each other. Nothing He made is incomplete—one thing helps explain and complete another. Who can fully understand the greatness of His glory?

Chapter 43

The bright sky is like a crown in the heavens, showing the beauty of creation in all its glory. When the sun rises, it announces the start of a new day. It is a stunning masterpiece made by the Most High. By midday, its heat dries the earth. Who can stand its blazing intensity? A person near a furnace feels extreme heat, but the sun's power is even greater, heating up mountains, sending out fiery rays, and shining so brightly that it dazzles and blinds the eyes.

How amazing is the Lord who created the sun! By His command, it moves quickly across the sky, completing its journey. The moon helps mark time, setting seasons and acting as a sign for the world. It signals special days and celebrations as its light grows and fades. The months are named after the moon, which follows its cycle of waxing and waning. It is one of the great lights in the heavens, shining beautifully in the sky.

The moon and stars sparkle like jewels, lighting up the heights of creation. At the Lord's command, they stay in perfect order, never failing in their purpose. Look at the rainbow and give praise to the One who made it. Its colors are breathtaking, stretching across the sky in a perfect arc, placed there by the hands of the Most High.

By His word, snow falls, and flashes of lightning carry out His will. He opens the skies, and clouds scatter like birds in flight. By His power, heavy clouds form, and hail falls when He commands. When He shows His presence, mountains tremble. At His word, warm winds blow. His thunder shakes the earth, and northern storms bring powerful winds. Snow falls gently like birds descending and covers the ground like swarms of locusts.

The brightness of snow catches the eye, filling hearts with wonder. Frost spreads across the land like salt, and icy landscapes sparkle like crystal. Cold winds freeze the waters, turning ponds and streams into solid ice. The cold burns the mountains, dries the wilderness, and scorches the grass like fire. But then mist rises to heal the earth, and after the heat, dew refreshes and cools the land.

With His wisdom, He calms the deep seas and places islands in their positions. Sailors who travel the oceans speak of its dangers, and we are amazed by the stories they tell. The sea is full of wonders—

creatures of all kinds, from the smallest to the largest, even massive sea monsters. At His command, His messengers complete their tasks, and by His word, everything stays in order.

Even if we spoke forever about His works, we could never fully describe them. All we can say is, "He is everything!" Who has the power to give Him the praise He truly deserves? He is greater than all He has created. The Lord is incredible beyond understanding. His power is more than we can imagine.

Praise the Lord and lift Him up as much as you can! Even then, He is greater than your praise. Give Him glory with all your strength and never stop, because no amount of praise will ever be enough. Who has seen Him completely to describe Him? Who can honor Him as He truly deserves? There is so much about Him we cannot see; we have only glimpsed a small part of His works. The Lord is the creator of all things, and He gives wisdom to those who honor Him.

Chapter 44

Let's take a moment to remember and honor the great people of the past—our ancestors from every generation. The Lord blessed them and showed His power through them since the beginning of time. Some were strong and wise rulers who led their nations with wisdom, gave good advice, and had great understanding. Others were prophets who spoke God's truth.

Some guided their people with wisdom, teaching them valuable lessons and sharing their knowledge. Their words were full of insight and instruction. Some used their creativity to make music and write poetry, expressing their thoughts beautifully. Others were gifted with wealth and skill, living peaceful and successful lives.

All of these people were respected while they lived and were admired in their time. Some left behind names that are still remembered today, and their praises continue to be spoken. But others have faded from history, as if they had never lived. They passed away without a lasting record, and so did their children after them.

Still, these were kind and compassionate people, and their good deeds will never be forgotten. Their legacy continues through their descendants, who remain part of God's covenant. Their families stand strong, and because of them, their lineage carries on. Their descendants will last for generations, and their honor will never fade.

Even though their bodies rest in peace, their names are remembered by those who come after them. People continue to celebrate their wisdom, and their praises are shared among the community.

Enoch pleased God and was taken up to heaven, serving as a lasting example of repentance. Noah was a good and righteous man. During a time of judgment, he saved humanity by building the ark, preserving life during the great flood. Because of him, God made an everlasting promise that the earth would never again be destroyed by a flood.

Abraham was a great leader, the father of many nations, unmatched in honor. He followed God's law and entered into a special covenant with Him. He kept his faith even when tested, proving his loyalty.

Because of this, God confirmed His promise to Abraham with an oath, saying that all nations would be blessed through his descendants. He promised to make Abraham's family as countless as the dust of the earth and the stars in the sky, giving them land stretching from sea to sea, from the Euphrates River to the farthest parts of the earth.

This promise was passed down to Isaac because of Abraham's faith, ensuring that the blessing and covenant would continue. That same blessing was given to Jacob, whom God chose and greatly favored. God gave Jacob an inheritance and divided it among the twelve tribes of Israel.

Chapter 45

God chose a man full of kindness and favor, someone loved by both Him and the people. That man was Moses, whose memory is forever honored. The Lord gave Moses great authority, placing him among His most faithful servants, and even lifted him up in front of his enemies. Through Moses, God performed amazing miracles and made him a leader who stood before kings. The Lord trusted him with His commandments and allowed him to experience a part of His divine presence.

Because of Moses' deep faith and humility, God set him apart from everyone else. The Lord spoke directly to him, allowed him to witness His power in the thick clouds, and gave him His laws face to face. These laws—the foundation of knowledge and life—were given to Moses to teach Jacob's descendants and to guide Israel in following God's ways.

God also chose Aaron, Moses' brother from the tribe of Levi, to serve as a holy priest. He made an everlasting covenant with Aaron, granting him the role of high priest for His people. Aaron was given great honor and dressed in sacred robes. His garments were beautifully made—fine linen, a long robe, and the ephod, all designed with skill. The hem of his robe had golden bells and pomegranates, so their sound could be heard in the temple, reminding Israel of God's presence.

Aaron wore special garments decorated with gold, blue, and purple, embroidered with great skill. He carried the Urim and Thummim, used for making judgments. His robe was woven with scarlet threads, and he wore gemstones engraved with the names of Israel's tribes, set in gold. On his turban was a golden crown with the words "HOLINESS," a symbol of honor, carefully crafted by skilled hands. Before Aaron, no one had ever worn such robes, and they were reserved for him and his descendants forever.

Aaron was responsible for offering daily sacrifices to God, twice a day without fail. Moses anointed Aaron with holy oil, dedicating him and his family to serve as priests for all time. Aaron was chosen to stand before the Lord, bless the people, and present offerings to God. Out of all the people, he alone was given the duty of offering sacrifices, burning incense, and making atonement for the nation.

The Lord gave Aaron the responsibility of teaching His laws and sharing His commands with Israel. However, in the wilderness, certain outsiders—Dathan, Abiram, and Korah's followers—grew jealous and rebelled against Aaron. Their actions angered the Lord, who responded with a powerful judgment, destroying them with fire and proving His authority.

Even after this, God continued to bless Aaron by granting him a special portion of Israel's offerings. He received the best of the people's harvests and was provided with food from the sacrifices. Aaron and his descendants were given their share from the offerings, just as God had commanded. However, Aaron did not receive a land inheritance like the other tribes, because the Lord Himself was his reward.

Phinehas, Aaron's grandson and the son of Eleazar, was greatly honored for standing up for God's covenant when the people turned away from Him. Because of Phinehas' actions, he helped restore

Israel's faith, and God made a lasting promise of peace with him. Phinehas was given leadership over the sanctuary and the people, and his descendants were promised the priesthood forever.

The Lord also made a covenant with David, the son of Jesse, from the tribe of Judah. The kingship was passed down through his descendants for generations. In the same way, Aaron's priesthood was preserved for his family line. May the Lord give you wisdom to lead His people with fairness, so they remain blessed and their honor lasts for generations to come.

Chapter 46

Joshua, the son of Nun, was a strong and courageous leader who followed Moses as a prophet. Just as his name means "salvation," he led God's people to victory, defeating their enemies and securing the land promised to Israel. How powerful he was when he lifted his hands and fought with his sword against cities! No one could stand as firm as Joshua because the Lord gave him victory over his enemies.

At his command, didn't the sun stop in the sky? Didn't one day seem to last twice as long? Surrounded by his enemies, Joshua called out to the Most High, and God answered him. The Lord sent massive hailstones to strike down the enemy, destroying those who fought against Him. Through these miracles, the nations saw the power of the Lord and realized that Joshua fought under God's guidance because he was faithful to Him.

Even during Moses' time, Joshua proved his loyalty. He and Caleb, the son of Jephunneh, stood against those who rebelled. They encouraged the people to trust in God and silenced their complaints. Out of the 600,000 Israelites who left Egypt, only Joshua and Caleb lived to enter the promised land, the land flowing with milk and honey. The Lord gave Caleb strength even in his old age, allowing him to conquer the hill country that became the inheritance of his descendants. This showed all of Israel that those who follow the Lord will be blessed.

The judges of Israel, whose names are remembered with honor, were those who remained faithful to God and kept their hearts pure. May their memory be cherished! May they rise again, and may their legacy continue through their children.

Samuel, the prophet of the Lord, was deeply loved by God and played a key role in choosing leaders for Israel. He ruled the nation according to God's law, and through him, the Lord watched over His people. Because of his faithfulness, Samuel proved to be a true prophet, and everything he spoke was confirmed by his visions.

When enemies surrounded Israel, Samuel cried out to the Lord and offered a lamb as a sacrifice. God answered him with a loud thunder from heaven, shaking the earth with His mighty voice. He struck down the rulers of the Tyrians and defeated the Philistine leaders.

Before he died, Samuel stood before the people and their king, declaring, "I have taken nothing from anyone—not even a sandal." No one could accuse him of wrongdoing. Even after his death, his prophetic words remained powerful. He predicted the downfall of the king and spoke from the grave, warning the people about their sins and calling them back to God.

Chapter 47

After him, Nathan became a prophet during David's reign. Just like the best part of an offering is set aside, David was chosen and set apart from the people of Israel. He fought lions as if they were goats and wrestled bears as if they were lambs.

As a young man, didn't David defeat a giant and remove the shame from his people? With just a sling, he struck down the proud Goliath. He called on the Most High, and God gave him the strength to defeat a mighty warrior and restore his nation's honor. The people celebrated his victories, praising him for the blessings of the Lord when a glorious crown was placed on his head.

David crushed his enemies from every side, defeating the Philistines and breaking their power so completely that it remains broken to this day. In everything he did, he gave thanks to the Holy One. He glorified God with his songs and poured his whole heart into praising his Creator.

He appointed singers to stand before the altar, filling the temple with beautiful music. He made the festivals more joyful and carefully planned times of worship to honor God's holy name. Their songs filled the sanctuary from early morning. The Lord forgave David's sins and strengthened him for all time. God made an everlasting covenant with him, ensuring that his descendants would rule from a glorious throne in Israel.

After David, his wise son took the throne, and because of David's faithfulness, this son ruled peacefully. Solomon's reign was marked by peace because the Lord gave him rest from his enemies. This gave Solomon the opportunity to build a temple for God's name and establish a sanctuary meant to last forever.

Solomon, how amazing was your wisdom when you were young! You were like an overflowing river of understanding. Your influence spread everywhere, filling the world with proverbs and wise sayings. Your reputation reached distant lands, and people admired you for the peace you brought to your kingdom. Nations were drawn to your songs, your proverbs, and your ability to explain mysteries.

By the power of the Lord, you gathered gold as if it were tin and silver as if it were as common as lead. But you let yourself be controlled by women, and they led you astray. Because of this, your honor was ruined, and your descendants became corrupted. Your actions brought God's anger upon your children. It is painful to see that your mistakes led to the division of the kingdom and the rise of rebellion in Ephraim.

Even so, the Lord did not take away His mercy. He did not destroy His people or erase the descendants of His chosen ones. He remained faithful to those who loved Him, keeping a remnant of Jacob's descendants and preserving a branch from David's family.

When Solomon died, his son Rehoboam took the throne, but he was foolish. His lack of wisdom embarrassed his people. His poor decisions caused the kingdom to rebel against him. Then came Jeroboam, the son of Nebat, who led Israel into sin, causing Ephraim to follow a corrupt path. Their sins kept increasing until they were finally removed from the land. They embraced all kinds of wickedness, and in the end, judgment came upon them.

Chapter 48

Elijah was a prophet whose presence burned like fire, and his words shone as brightly as a torch. Because of his deep passion for God, he brought famine to the land and reduced the number of its people. By the Lord's command, he stopped the rain, and three times, fire came down from heaven at his word.

Elijah, your deeds were truly amazing! Who could compare to you? You brought the dead back to life, saving them from the grave by the power of the Most High. You overthrew kings and healed the sick. You heard God's voice at Mount Sinai and received His commands at Horeb. You anointed kings to carry out justice and appointed prophets to continue your mission.

You were taken up to heaven in a whirlwind, riding a chariot pulled by fiery horses. Your name was meant to bring correction at the right time, to calm God's anger before it fully erupted, to bring peace between fathers and sons, and to restore the tribes of Israel. Blessed are those who saw your greatness and experienced your kindness—they were truly fortunate.

Elijah was carried away in a whirlwind, and his spirit was passed down to Elisha. Elisha was fearless, and no ruler could stand against him. Nothing was too difficult for him. Even after his death, his power continued, and miracles still happened because of him. His life was full of wonders, and even after he was gone, his deeds amazed people.

But despite these incredible signs, the people did not change. They refused to turn from their sins until they were defeated and taken captive, scattered across different lands. Only a small group remained, led by a ruler from David's family. Some of them did what was right, but many continued to do wrong.

Hezekiah strengthened his city and built a water system. He cut through solid rock with iron tools and made reservoirs to store water. During his reign, Sennacherib invaded and sent his commander, Rabshakeh, who spoke arrogantly and threatened Zion. The people were terrified, as if they were in the pains of childbirth.

But they cried out to the merciful Lord, lifting their hands in prayer. The Holy One heard them from heaven and rescued them through the prophet Isaiah. God struck down the Assyrian army, and His angel wiped them out completely. Hezekiah pleased the Lord by following the ways of his ancestor David, listening to the guidance of Isaiah the prophet, who was wise and faithful in his visions.

During Hezekiah's time, the sun moved backward, and his life was extended. Isaiah, filled with a remarkable spirit, saw visions of the future and brought comfort to those grieving in Zion. He revealed events that would happen, even to the end of time, showing hidden things before they took place.

Chapter 49

The memory of Josiah is like a sweet-smelling incense, carefully crafted by a skilled maker. His goodness was as delightful as honey on the tongue and as joyful as music at a celebration. Josiah did what was right, leading the people back to God and removing sinful practices from the land. He devoted himself fully to serving the Lord and stayed faithful, even when the world around him was filled with corruption.

Unlike David, Hezekiah, and Josiah, most of the other kings of Judah turned away from God's laws. Because of their wickedness, they lost their thrones, and foreign nations took over their kingdom. Strangers ruled over them, and their honor was stripped away. They burned down the holy city and left its streets empty, just as the prophet Jeremiah had warned.

Jeremiah was chosen by God before he was even born. Though he faced much suffering, he was called to deliver God's message—to tear down and destroy what was wrong but also to rebuild and restore what was good. Ezekiel, another great prophet, was given a vision of God's glory. He saw the Lord's presence through the chariot of the cherubim. He spoke of God's judgment on enemies and brought blessings to those who followed the right path.

May the bones of the twelve prophets rest in peace, for they gave hope and courage to the people of Israel. How can we ever give enough praise to Zerubbabel? He was like a seal on God's right hand, chosen for a special purpose. The same can be said of Jesus, the son of Josedek, who helped rebuild the Lord's temple and guided the people back to holiness, preparing them for eternal glory.

Nehemiah also deserves great honor. He restored the broken walls of the city, rebuilt its gates, and gave the people back their homes. No one on earth has ever been like Enoch, who was taken up from the earth. No one has been like Joseph, who became a leader and protector of his people. Even after his death, his bones were treated with the highest respect.

Shem and Seth were greatly honored among men, but above all creation, Adam was set apart.

Chapter 50

Simon, son of Onias, was a high priest who dedicated his life to restoring God's temple and making it stronger. During his time, he built up the foundations, reinforced the double walls, and raised the great enclosures of the temple. He also oversaw the construction of a huge water reservoir and a massive bronze basin as wide as the sea. He worked hard to protect his people from disaster and fortified the city so it could withstand enemy attacks.

How magnificent he was when he appeared before the people, stepping out from behind the temple's veil! He shined like the morning star breaking through the clouds, like the full moon glowing at its brightest, and like the sun beaming over the Lord's temple. He was as stunning as a rainbow in the clouds, as beautiful as roses blooming in early spring, as fresh as lilies by a flowing stream, and as fragrant as a tree full of frankincense in summer. He was like the bright fire of burning incense, like a golden bowl covered in shining jewels, like an olive tree heavy with fruit, and like a tall cypress tree reaching into the sky.

When Simon wore his sacred robes, dressed in all his splendor, and stepped up to the holy altar, the sanctuary seemed to glow with glory. As he received offerings from the priests, standing with his fellow ministers like a wreath surrounding him, he was as majestic as a cedar tree in Lebanon, standing tall among towering palm trees. The priests, the sons of Aaron, stood in their sacred garments, holding the Lord's offerings before the entire assembly of Israel.

When the service at the altar was finished, Simon carefully arranged the offering for the Almighty. He lifted his hands to the cup of wine and poured it at the base of the altar as a sweet offering to the King of all. Then the sons of Aaron sounded the trumpets of hammered silver, their music filling the air to honor the Most High.

The people bowed low in worship, pressing their faces to the ground before the Almighty God. The singers raised their voices in praise, and the entire temple was filled with the sound of beautiful music. The people cried out to the Lord, calling upon His mercy, and they remained in prayer until the sacred ceremony was complete.

Afterward, Simon stepped down and raised his hands over the entire congregation of Israel, blessing them in the name of the Lord and lifting up His holy name. He bowed again in worship and declared a blessing from the Most High:

"Let us bless the God of all, who performs wonders everywhere, who formed us in the womb and continues to show us His kindness. May He fill our hearts with joy and grant us peace in Israel for all generations. May His mercy be with us, and may He save us at the perfect time."

My soul is troubled by two nations, and there is a third that I don't even consider a nation: those who live on the mountains of Samaria, the Philistines, and the foolish people of Shechem.

I, Jesus, the son of Sirach, Eleazar of Jerusalem, have written this book filled with wisdom and understanding, sharing knowledge from my heart. Blessed is the one who follows these teachings. Whoever treasures them will grow wise, and by putting them into practice, they will gain strength in all things. The light of the Lord will guide their path.

Chapter 51

A Prayer of Jesus, the son of Sirach.

I thank you, Lord, my King, and I praise you, my God and Savior. I am grateful for your name because you have always protected and helped me. You have saved me from danger and rescued me from the lies and traps of those who spread false stories. You stood by my side, saving me with your endless mercy and the power of your name.

You delivered me from those who were ready to attack me, from people who wanted to harm me. You saved me from many troubles, from the fire that surrounded me, and from flames I did not cause. You pulled me back from the edge of death, from false accusations and the words of those who slandered me in front of the king.

My soul was close to death, and my life was nearly over. I was trapped on all sides, and no one could help me. I looked for someone to save me, but there was no one. Then I remembered your mercy, Lord, and your promises that last forever. You save those who wait for you and protect them from their enemies.

I lifted my prayer from the earth, begging to be rescued from death. I called on the Lord, the Father of my Lord, asking Him not to leave me alone in my time of trouble, when no one else would stand up for me. I will praise your name forever and sing songs of thanks because you heard my prayer.

You saved me from destruction and delivered me in my darkest moments. Because of this, I will praise you, bless your name, and glorify the Lord.

When I was young, before I had much experience, I searched for wisdom through prayer. I asked for her guidance near the temple, and I will continue to seek her until my last day.

From my early days until now, my heart has been filled with joy because of wisdom. I have walked with honesty and followed her path since my youth. By listening carefully, I gained great wisdom for myself. She has been a great benefit to me, and I will give glory to the one who gives wisdom.

I was determined to follow her, eager to do what is good, and I have no regrets. My soul struggled to gain her, and I worked hard in my efforts. I lifted my hands to heaven and grieved over my lack of understanding. I focused my heart on wisdom, and in purity, I found her. From the beginning, I dedicated myself to her, and because of this, I will never be abandoned.

I faced many struggles in my search for wisdom, but in return, I found something priceless. The Lord rewarded me with the gift of speech, and I will use it to praise Him.

Come close to me, all who lack understanding, and make your home in the house of wisdom. Why do you still lack what you need? Your souls thirst deeply for wisdom. I opened my mouth and said, "Gain wisdom without spending money. Take her teachings upon yourself, and let your soul embrace her instruction. She is easy to find.

See for yourselves that I put in only a little effort, but I gained much peace. Seek wisdom as if you were buying silver, and through her, you will receive wealth greater than gold. Let your soul rejoice in the Lord's mercy, and never be ashamed to praise Him.

Complete your work before your time runs out, and at the right moment, He will reward you."

Wisdom of Solomon

Chapter 1

Love what is right, all of you who lead and judge others. Keep your thoughts pure and seek the Lord with a sincere heart. He makes Himself known to those who trust Him and allows Himself to be found by those who truly want to understand Him.

Wrong thinking leads people away from God, and those who try to challenge Him will be proven foolish. Wisdom cannot stay with someone who chooses evil, and it cannot live in a body controlled by sin.

A spirit that is holy and disciplined avoids lies, rejects foolish thinking, and stays far from wrongdoing. Wisdom is a gift that helps people, but it does not ignore those who speak against God. He sees what is in every heart and knows our deepest thoughts.

The Spirit of the Lord fills the whole world, holds everything together, and hears every word spoken. No one who speaks dishonestly can hide, and justice will not let them go unpunished.

Wicked people will be exposed by their actions, and the words they speak will reach God, revealing their wrongdoing. Nothing is truly hidden—every whisper is heard, and no secret escapes His attention.

Be careful not to complain needlessly or speak badly about others. Every word matters, and lies can destroy a soul. Do not bring harm upon yourself by choosing the wrong path, and do not invite destruction through your actions.

God did not create death, and He does not take pleasure in seeing people suffer. Everything He made was meant to thrive, and the forces of nature were created without destruction in them. Righteousness leads to eternal life.

But the wicked bring death upon themselves through their choices and words. They treat it like a friend, wasting their lives and forming a bond with it. Through their actions, they show that they belong to its power.

Chapter 2

Their way of thinking was completely wrong, yet they convinced themselves:

"Life is short and full of trouble. There's no way to escape death, and no one has ever come back from the grave.

We were born by accident, and when we die, it will be as if we never existed. Our breath disappears like smoke, and our thoughts are just tiny sparks that flicker for a moment.

When that spark dies out, our bodies turn to dust, and our spirits vanish like the wind.

As time passes, people will forget our names, and everything we did will be erased. Our lives will disappear like a passing cloud or vanish like mist under the heat of the sun.

Our time on earth is like a shadow that quickly fades, and nothing can stop the end from coming.

So, let's enjoy life while we can. Let's take in all the pleasures of the world while we're still young.

We'll drink the finest wine and enjoy the sweetest perfumes. We won't miss a single moment to admire the beauty of spring.

We'll make ourselves crowns of flowers before they wilt and make sure we experience every desire we have.

We'll leave our mark wherever we go because this is what we deserve—this is the life we were meant to live.

Let's take advantage of the weak, show no kindness to widows, and ignore the wisdom of the elderly.

Only power matters—if you're weak, you're useless.

Let's go after the righteous man because he's a problem for us. He challenges our actions, calls us lawbreakers, and points out that we don't even follow our own rules.

He claims to know God and even calls himself a child of the Lord.

He looks down on us and refuses to live as we do, saying our ways are wrong. He insists that good people will have a happy ending and proudly declares that God is his father.

Let's test him to see if he's telling the truth. Let's find out what happens to him in the end.

If he really is a child of God, then God will protect him and keep him from harm.

Let's insult him and make him suffer to see how patient and humble he really is.

Let's give him a shameful death and see if God saves him, just like he claims."

This is how they thought, but they were completely wrong. Their own evil blinded them.

They didn't understand God's ways or believe in the rewards of living a good life. They had no idea what was in store for those who live with honesty and faith.

God created people to live forever and made them in His own image.

But death entered the world because of the devil's jealousy, and only those who follow him will experience it.

Chapter 3

The souls of good and faithful people are safe with God, and nothing can harm them. To those who don't understand, their death might look like a terrible loss. It may seem like their lives ended in failure, but the truth is—they are at peace.

Even if it looks like they suffered, their future is full of hope because they will live forever. After going through a short time of testing, they will receive amazing rewards. God examined them and saw that they were worthy of Him.

He purified them, just like gold is refined in fire, and accepted them as a perfect offering. When their reward comes, they will shine brightly and move like sparks through dry grass.

They will rule over nations and lead people, and the Lord will always be their King.

Those who trust in Him will understand the truth, and those who remain loyal will live with Him in love, because He shows kindness and mercy to those He has chosen.

But those who live without God will be judged for their actions and thoughts. They turned away from what is right and refused to follow the Lord.

People who reject wisdom and discipline bring misery upon themselves. Their hopes are empty, their hard work leads to nothing, and everything they try to accomplish will fail.

Their wives will act foolishly, their children will follow in their wicked ways, and their entire family line will be ruined.

On the other hand, a woman who has done no wrong, even if she has no children, is blessed. She will be joyful when God judges all people and gives out His rewards.

A man who stays faithful, avoids sin, and keeps his heart pure before the Lord is also blessed. He will receive great rewards and a joyful place among God's people.

Doing what is right will always bring honor, and a life built on wisdom will never fall apart.

But children born from unfaithful relationships will struggle. The children of sin will eventually fade away.

Even if they live a long time, they will not be respected, and their old age will bring them no dignity.

If they die young, they will have no hope or comfort when they stand before God.

A family that comes from evil and dishonesty will always face sorrow and hardship.

Chapter 4

It is far better to live a good and honorable life, even without children, because doing what is right brings lasting value. A good life is remembered by both God and people. It inspires others while it lasts, and when it is gone, people long for it to return. It moves through time with honor, achieving rewards that are pure and everlasting.

But the many descendants of wicked people bring no real benefit. The children of those who live without goodness will not take root or last. Even if they seem to grow for a little while, they will be weak and easily blown away like dust in the wind. Strong storms will rip them from the ground completely.

Their branches will snap before they fully grow, and their fruit will be worthless—unfit to eat or use for anything good. Children born from sinful acts will stand as proof of their parents' wrongdoings when the time comes for judgment.

But a good person, even if they die young, will find peace. True honor in life isn't about how many years a person lives or how much time passes. Instead, wisdom is like gray hair for the soul, and a pure life is just as valuable as growing old.

A person who pleases God is deeply loved by Him. When they live among those who do wrong, God takes them away to protect them from harm.

They are removed before evil can corrupt their heart or before lies can lead them astray. Wickedness has a way of darkening even the brightest soul, and uncontrolled desires can mislead even the purest heart.

A life that reaches its purpose quickly is just as meaningful as a long one. The soul of a good person brings joy to the Lord, so He takes them away from the corruption around them.

Those who see this happening don't understand. They don't realize that God shows love and mercy to those He has chosen and that He watches over those who live in holiness.

Even after death, a good person's life will stand as a reminder to those who live in wickedness. A young person who lives with wisdom and goodness will reveal the flaws of an old person who has spent their years doing wrong.

The ungodly will see the end of a wise person's life but won't understand what God had planned or why He protected them.

They will see, but instead of learning from it, they will be filled with resentment. And just as they rejected wisdom, the Lord will turn away from them.

In the end, they will be nothing but dishonored bodies, a disgrace among the dead.

God will bring them down, leaving them speechless and trembling. Their lives will fall apart, leaving them in misery, and their names will soon be forgotten.

When the time comes for their sins to be counted, fear will consume them. Their own actions will be the proof against them, standing as witnesses to all the wrong they have done.

Chapter 5

The good and faithful will stand tall and unshaken in front of those who once mistreated them and thought they were worthless. When their enemies see them, they will be filled with fear and shock, completely stunned by the unexpected sight of their victory.

Full of regret, they will whisper to each other, saying, "Is this really the person we used to mock? The one we laughed at and thought was foolish? We believed their life had no meaning and that their death was a disgrace.

But now, look at them! How did they become part of God's people? How are they counted among those who are holy?

We were the ones who were blind and foolish. We strayed far from the truth. We never found the light of righteousness, and we lived without real direction.

Instead of following what was right, we chased after destruction. We ignored the ways of the Lord and spent our lives lost and wandering.

What did we gain from our pride? What good did our wealth and bragging bring us? Nothing. Everything we built disappeared in an instant, like a shadow passing by or a gust of wind that leaves no trace.

It's like a ship sailing through rough waters—once it's gone, there's no sign it was ever there, no mark left on the waves.

Or like a bird flying across the sky—the air moves for a moment as its wings pass through, but once it's gone, there's no proof it was ever there.

Or like an arrow shot from a bow—the air parts briefly, but it quickly comes back together, leaving no sign of the arrow's flight.

In the same way, we lived our lives and disappeared without a trace. We left nothing good behind because we were consumed by our own wrongdoings."

The hopes of the wicked are weak and fragile—like dust blown away by the wind, or foam that disappears in a storm. Their memories fade like smoke drifting in the air or like a visitor who stays only for a short while before being forgotten.

But those who have lived righteously will live forever, receiving their reward from the Lord Himself. The Most High will care for them and bless them with eternal life.

They will be crowned with glory, and the Lord will personally place a royal crown upon their heads. He will protect them and cover them with His power.

God will prepare for battle, wrapping Himself in passion like armor, using all of creation as His weapon to bring justice against His enemies.

Righteousness will be His chest plate, and fairness will be His helmet.

He will hold holiness as a shield and sharpen His burning anger like a sword.

All of creation will join Him in the fight, standing with Him against those who oppose Him.

Lightning bolts will strike with perfect aim, flashing down like arrows fired from a skilled archer's bow.

Hailstones will fall like deadly weapons, crashing down with unstoppable force. The waters of the sea will rise up in fury, and rivers will overflow, sweeping away His enemies.

A powerful wind will come like a storm, scattering them and leaving nothing behind.

Their wickedness will bring destruction upon the earth, and their corruption will cause even the mightiest thrones to collapse.

Chapter 6

Listen, kings, and pay attention. Listen carefully, rulers of the earth. Hear this, you who govern many people and take pride in ruling over countless nations.

Your power comes from the Lord, and your authority is given by the Most High. One day, He will hold you accountable for how you used it and ask about the choices you made.

You were meant to lead with fairness, but instead, you failed to bring justice and did not follow God's ways.

Because of this, He will judge you swiftly and without hesitation. Those in power will face a stricter judgment.

Ordinary people may find mercy and forgiveness, but leaders will be held to a higher standard and judged more seriously.

The Lord of all does not show favoritism. He is not influenced by status or impressed by power because He created both the mighty and the weak, and He cares for everyone equally.

But those who have been given greater responsibility will face greater scrutiny.

These words are for you, rulers, so that you may learn wisdom and stay on the right path.

Those who respect what is holy will be blessed, and those who seek wisdom will learn how to defend what is right.

Desire wisdom and treasure her, rulers, and she will guide you.

Wisdom shines brightly and never fails. She is easy to find for those who love her and reveals herself to those who seek her.

She makes herself known to those who long for her and eagerly comes to those who desire her.

Anyone who searches for wisdom early in the morning will find her waiting at their doorstep, ready to be embraced.

Thinking about wisdom brings complete understanding, and staying focused on her removes all worries.

Wisdom searches for those who are worthy of her. She shows herself to them and gently guides their every choice.

The first step toward wisdom is wanting to learn, and the love of learning leads to a desire for understanding.

Loving wisdom means following her ways, and keeping her ways leads to eternal life.

Eternal life brings a person closer to God.

So, the pursuit of wisdom leads to the path of a lasting kingdom.

If you desire power and authority, rulers of the earth, seek wisdom, and you will rule wisely forever.

I will reveal what wisdom is and where she comes from. I will not keep her secrets hidden but will share her knowledge for all to understand. I will not withhold the truth.

I refuse to let jealousy consume me because envy cannot exist alongside wisdom.

A nation guided by wisdom brings safety to the world, and a wise leader provides stability to his people.

So listen closely to my words, accept this teaching, and you will gain great wisdom.

Chapter 7

I am human, just like everyone else—a descendant of the first person formed from the earth. My body took shape over ten months in my mother's womb, nourished by her blood, created through human life and the bond of marriage.

When I was born, I breathed the same air as everyone else and rested on the same ground. Like all newborns, I cried out with my first voice. I was cared for, wrapped in soft cloth, and nurtured.

No king is born differently, for every person enters life in the same way and leaves it in the same way.

Knowing this, I prayed, and I was given understanding. I asked, and wisdom was given to me.

I valued her more than power and riches, and wealth meant nothing to me compared to her.

I didn't see her as less important than the most valuable gems, because next to her, gold is like a handful of dust, and silver is no more than clay.

I loved her more than health and beauty and chose her over even the brightest light because her glow never fades.

With her came every good thing, and in her hands were endless treasures.

I rejoiced in them all because wisdom guided them, though at first, I didn't realize she was the source of them all.

I gained wisdom honestly and now share what I've learned freely, hiding nothing from others.

She is an endless treasure for those who embrace her, and through her, they build a close relationship with God, who praises them for the gifts they share through wisdom.

May God grant me the ability to speak wisely and think thoughts that reflect the wisdom I've been given, for He leads wisdom and corrects those who seek understanding.

Both we and our words are in His hands, as well as all knowledge and the ability to create and build.

He gave me deep understanding of the universe and how everything in it works together.

I know how time unfolds—the past, present, and future—the changes of the seasons, and the cycles of the years.

I have learned about the movement of stars, the nature of living creatures, the instincts of wild animals, the force of the wind, and the thoughts in human hearts.

I understand the variety of plants and the hidden powers of their roots.

I have been taught all things, both seen and unseen, because wisdom, the designer of all creation, has been my teacher.

Wisdom is a spirit that is intelligent, holy, one of a kind, subtle, free-moving, clear in speech, pure, strong, and always seeking what is good.

She is sharp, unhindered, kind, devoted to people, steady, unwavering, free from worry, powerful, all-seeing, and able to move through all minds that are wise, pure, and open.

She moves more smoothly than anything else and touches everything because of her purity.

She is the breath of God's power, a shining reflection of His glory. Nothing corrupt can enter her.

She is the light of eternity, a perfect mirror of God's work, and an image of His goodness.

Though she is one, she can do all things. She remains unchanged while renewing all things. She enters the hearts of good people in every generation, making them close to God and guiding them as His messengers.

God loves no one more than those who welcome wisdom into their lives.

She is more beautiful than the sun and shines brighter than all the stars. Her light is greater than even the brightest day.

For while daylight fades into night, wisdom can never be overcome by darkness.

Chapter 8

Her wisdom reaches across the entire universe, guiding everything with perfect order and balance. From a young age, I loved her deeply and longed to make her my companion. Her beauty and goodness completely captivated me.

She shows her greatness by staying close to God, and He treasures her above all things. She has a deep understanding of God and works in perfect harmony with His plans.

If wealth is something to be desired, then what could be richer than wisdom, which creates all things? If understanding is what we seek, who is wiser than the one who designed the universe?

If someone values goodness, wisdom produces it in abundance. She teaches self-control, insight, fairness, and courage—the most important qualities anyone can have.

If experience is what matters, wisdom holds knowledge of the past and can reveal what is to come. She understands every language, explains mysteries, and reveals hidden truths. She knows how the seasons change and can predict events before they happen.

This is why I chose to make her my guide, knowing she would lead me with wisdom and support me through every challenge and difficulty.

With her by my side, I will earn honor among great crowds and gain the respect of elders, even while I am still young.

People will recognize my sound judgment and respect me in the presence of rulers.

When I remain silent, others will wait eagerly for my words. When I begin to speak, they will listen closely. If I continue, they will be drawn in, holding back their own words just to hear more.

With wisdom, I will achieve a lasting legacy, and my name will be remembered for generations.

I will have the power to govern nations and lead many people.

Even the strongest rulers will hear my name and feel awe. Among the people, I will be celebrated for my kindness and praised for my courage in times of trouble.

And when I return home, wisdom will bring me peace. Conversations with her are never dull, and her presence fills life with joy and satisfaction.

As I thought about all of this—how wisdom leads to a fulfilling life, how her friendship brings true happiness, how her efforts create lasting success, how she grants deep understanding, and how her words bring honor—I decided I had to seek her with all my heart.

Even as a child, I had a curious mind and a good heart.

Or maybe, because I tried to be good, I was given the gift of a pure soul.

But I realized that wisdom could not truly be mine unless God gave her to me. I understood that this kind of insight comes only from Him.

So, I turned my heart toward God, and with complete sincerity, I prayed to Him and begged for His guidance.

Chapter 9

O Lord, God of my ancestors, the source of all mercy,
You spoke the world into existence with just Your word.
With Your wisdom, You created humanity,
Giving them the responsibility to care for Your creation,
To lead with justice and truth,
And to judge fairly with honest and pure hearts.

Please give me wisdom, the one who stands beside You.
Do not leave me out from among Your faithful servants.

I am Your servant, the child of Your handmaid,
  A mortal being, weak and short-lived,
  Lacking full understanding of justice and truth.

Even if a person is seen as perfect,
  Without Your wisdom, they are nothing.
You have chosen me to lead Your people,
  To guide the sons and daughters of Israel.
You have commanded me to build a sacred temple on Your holy
  mountain,
  An altar in the city where You dwell,
  A reflection of the holy place You established long ago.

Wisdom is with You and knows all that You do.
She was there when You created the world.
She understands what pleases You
  And what is right according to Your commands.

Send her down from Your holy dwelling,
  Let her come from Your glorious throne.
Let her be by my side to guide me,
  So that I may do what is right in Your eyes.

She knows all things and leads with great wisdom.
She will show me the right way to act
  And protect me with her shining light.
With her, my actions will be just,
  I will lead Your people with fairness,
And I will be worthy to continue my father's work.

Who can truly understand Your plans, O God?
Who can know what You desire?

Human thoughts are fragile,
    And our plans often fail.
Our bodies weigh down our souls,
    And our earthly worries cloud our minds.

We struggle to understand even the things close to us,
    So how can we possibly understand the things of heaven?
Who could know Your will unless You give them wisdom
    And send Your Holy Spirit from above?

Wisdom is the one who guides people on earth,
    Through her, we learn what pleases You,
    And through her, we are saved.

Chapter 10

Wisdom protected the first father of the world, watching over him until the end. Though he was created alone, wisdom saved him from his mistakes and gave him the power to rule over all creation.

But when a wicked man turned away from wisdom in anger, he brought destruction upon himself. His rage led him to commit the worst sin—killing his own brother.

When the world was filled with evil, and a great flood came, wisdom stepped in again. She guided the one righteous man who was saved in a small wooden ark.

Later, when people united in rebellion and were scattered in confusion, wisdom recognized the righteous man among them. She kept him pure before God and gave him strength when he felt the pain of losing his child.

When the ungodly faced destruction, wisdom rescued the one righteous man who escaped the fiery judgment that fell on five sinful cities.

Their sin is still remembered today—through the smoking wasteland that remains, the fruit that looks good but never ripens, and the pillar of salt standing as a reminder of their disbelief.

By rejecting wisdom, they lost all sense of what is good and left behind a lasting sign of their foolishness. Their downfall serves as a warning for all time.

But wisdom always saves those who trust in her and rescues them from harm.

When a righteous man fled from his brother's anger, wisdom guided him in the right direction. She taught him God's ways and helped him understand sacred truths. She blessed his hard work and made his efforts successful.

When greed led others to mistreat him, wisdom stood by his side and turned his struggles into success.

She protected him from his enemies, ruined the plans of those who tried to harm him, and proved that righteousness is stronger than any earthly power.

When a good man was sold into slavery, wisdom never left him. She kept him from sin, stayed with him even in the darkness of the prison, and gave him strength through his chains.

She remained with him until he was freed and brought to a throne, giving him power over those who had once oppressed him. She exposed the lies of his enemies and gave him lasting honor.

Wisdom saved an innocent people, rescuing a holy generation from the hands of those who enslaved them.

She entered the heart of a faithful servant of God, giving him the courage to stand against mighty kings with signs and miracles.

She rewarded the righteous, led them on an incredible journey, protected them during the day, and became a pillar of fire to guide them at night.

She safely brought them across the Red Sea and through the deep waters.

But she destroyed their enemies, drowning them in the sea.

The righteous took the wealth of the wicked and lifted their voices in praise, honoring Your holy name, Lord. They sang songs to celebrate Your mighty hand, which fought for them.

For wisdom gave speech to those who could not speak and even gave infants the ability to speak clearly.

Chapter 11

Wisdom guided a holy prophet, making sure everything he did was successful. She led the people safely through a dry and empty desert, where they set up camp in unfamiliar land.

They stood strong against their enemies and pushed back those who tried to harm them.

When they became thirsty, they cried out to You, and You answered by bringing water from a solid rock. Streams flowed from stone, giving them life.

What had been a punishment for their enemies became a blessing for Your people in their time of need.

While their enemies suffered as rivers turned into thick, clotted blood—punishment for ordering the deaths of infants—You gave

Your people an endless supply of fresh water, more than they ever expected.

By letting them experience thirst, You showed them how severe their enemies' punishment really was.

When Your people were tested, You corrected them gently with kindness and mercy. But the ungodly faced harsh judgment, suffering greatly.

You disciplined Your people like a loving father, but You punished their enemies like a strict judge handing down a sentence.

No matter where their enemies were—near or far—they all suffered the same.

They grieved and groaned as they remembered the past.

When they saw how their suffering had turned into a blessing for others, they started to understand Your power.

They no longer mocked the one they had once rejected.

In the end, they were filled with awe. Their thirst was nothing like that of the righteous.

Because of their foolishness in worshiping useless animals and lowly creatures, You sent swarms of mindless beasts to punish them.

Through this, You taught them that people are often punished by the very things they sin with.

Your mighty hand, which shaped the world from nothing, was not limited in its power. You could have sent fierce bears, roaring lions,

or newly created, unknown beasts filled with rage—breathing fire, blowing smoke, and flashing sparks from their eyes.

These creatures could have destroyed through sheer violence, but their presence alone would have been terrifying.

Yet, You didn't need them. With just a single breath, You could have wiped them out.

Justice would have chased them down, scattering them like dust in the wind with the power of Your might.

But You, in Your wisdom, balance all things perfectly, measuring them with precision.

Your strength is unshakable and cannot be challenged. Who could stand against the power of Your arm?

To You, the entire world is as small as a grain of sand on a scale or a drop of morning dew on the ground.

Yet, despite all Your power, You show mercy to everything, because You can do all things.

Instead of destroying people for their sins, You give them time to turn back to You.

You love everything You have made and hate nothing, for if You despised it, it wouldn't even exist.

If You had not wanted it to be, how could anything have survived? How could anything continue without Your command?

You protect all living things because they belong to You, O Lord, the One who loves all life.

Chapter 12

Your perfect spirit is present in everything.

You gently correct those who go astray, reminding them of their mistakes so they can turn away from evil and believe in You, Lord.

The people who first lived in Your sacred land did terrible things. They practiced magic, performed unholy rituals, and had no mercy.

They sacrificed their own children, ate human flesh and blood, and made alliances based on evil. They even killed innocent infants.

You commanded their destruction through our ancestors so that the land, which is precious to You, could be given to people who would honor and serve You.

Still, You treated even these wicked people with some mercy, recognizing them as human beings. Instead of wiping them out all at once, You sent hornets to slowly drive them away.

It wasn't because You lacked the power to destroy them instantly. With one word, You could have sent mighty warriors or fierce creatures to wipe them out.

But You judged them gradually, giving them a chance to change, even though You knew their hearts were corrupt from the start and unlikely to turn to You.

From the beginning, they were destined for destruction. You didn't ignore their sins out of fear of anyone.

Who could question Your actions and ask, "Why did You do this?"

Who could argue against Your decisions or claim You were unfair for removing nations that had become unworthy?

Who could defend such evil people before You?

There is no other god besides You, the one who cares for all creation. No one can say that Your judgments are unjust.

No king or ruler can stand against You or overturn what You decide.

You are just and rule everything with fairness, never punishing someone who doesn't deserve it.

Your strength is the foundation of Your justice, and because You have complete authority, You are patient with us.

When people doubt Your power, You show them Your strength and humble those who question You.

Yet, even with all Your power, You judge with kindness and lead with great patience, acting at the time You choose.

Through this, You taught Your people that true justice should also come with kindness.

You gave Your children hope, showing them that You always provide a chance to repent when they sin.

If You were patient with the enemies of Your people—those who deserved destruction—giving them time to turn from evil,

how much more carefully do You judge Your own children, to whom You made promises through their ancestors?

When You discipline us, You are even harsher with our enemies, teaching us to recognize Your goodness when we judge and to seek Your mercy when we are judged.

The wicked, who lived foolishly, were punished through their own sinful ways.

They strayed far from the truth, worshiping animals as gods—creatures even their enemies found shameful. They were misled and acted like senseless children.

So, You judged them in a way that matched their own foolishness, treating them as they behaved—like ignorant children.

Those who ignored Your gentle warnings eventually faced the full punishment they deserved.

Through the very creatures they worshiped as gods, they suffered, and in their pain, they finally recognized the one true God they had once rejected.

In the end, their guilt was undeniable, and their punishment was just.

Chapter 13

All those who did not understand God were naturally unwise. They failed to recognize the One who created everything, even though His existence was clear in the world around them. They could not see the Creator through the beauty of His works.

Instead, they believed that fire, wind, the air, the stars, the raging seas, or the bright lights in the sky were gods that ruled over the earth.

If they thought these things were gods because of how beautiful they were, they should have realized that the One who created them must be even greater, for He is the true source of beauty.

And if they were amazed by the power of nature, they should have understood that the Creator is far mightier.

The greatness and beauty of creation give us a glimpse of the One who made them all.

Still, these people deserve only some blame, for perhaps they were searching for God and got lost along the way.

They carefully studied His creation, using their senses to admire the wonders of the world.

But even then, they have no excuse.

If they had enough intelligence to study the universe and its mysteries, how did they fail to find the One who created it all?

Instead, they placed their trust in lifeless things, calling them gods—objects made by human hands from gold and silver, shaped to look like animals or carved from stone by ancient craftsmen.

For example, a woodworker cuts down a tree that is easy to shape. He strips off its bark and carves it into something useful for his daily life.

The leftover wood he burns to cook his meals and satisfy his hunger.

Then, using a rough piece of wood that is full of knots, he carves it with little effort, shaping it with the skills he has learned in his free time. He might make it look like a person or even a small animal. He paints it red, covering its flaws with dye.

After finishing, he finds a place for it, fixing it to a wall and securing it with iron so that it won't fall over, knowing it is too weak to stand on its own.

Even though he knows it is just a piece of wood, he prays to it for blessings on his home, his marriage, and his children.

He asks a lifeless object to give him good health. He seeks life from something that is dead.

He begs for help from something that has no understanding.

For a safe journey, he looks for guidance from something that cannot take a single step.

And for success in his work and business, he puts his trust in something with hands that cannot move.

Chapter 14

Someone preparing to sail across dangerous seas puts their trust in a piece of wood, even though the wood itself is weaker than the ship that carries them.

Ships were created because people wanted to make money, and it was human skill and wisdom that shaped them.

But, O Father, it is You who truly guides their journey. You created paths in the sea and set a course through the waves.

This shows that You can save people from any danger, even allowing those with no experience to travel safely across the waters.

You designed everything with purpose, and as a result, people trust their lives to fragile boats and rafts, yet they make it through stormy seas unharmed.

Long ago, when the proud giants of old were wiped out, the future of the world was saved on a simple wooden ark, and it was Your hand that led humanity forward.

Blessed is the wood that serves a good purpose,

but cursed is the idol made by human hands, along with the one who created it.

For an object shaped by human effort should never be called a god.

God hates both wickedness and those who practice it.

He will judge both the act and the person who commits it.

This is why the idols worshiped by nations will face judgment. Even though they are made from materials God created, they have become disgusting, trapping people in lies and leading the foolish astray.

Idolatry was the beginning of sin, and from it, corruption spread into the world.

These false gods were never part of creation from the start, and they will not last forever.

They were made because of human arrogance, and their end is already decided.

For example, a grieving father, heartbroken over the loss of a child, might carve a statue to look like his son or daughter. Over time, he begins to treat this lifeless figure as if it were real, eventually setting up rituals to honor it.

Before long, others follow his example, and the false practice grows into a tradition.

Soon, rulers give orders that these statues should be respected as gods.

When people cannot honor their rulers in person because they live far away, they create statues to represent them. Through these images, they try to show devotion as if the ruler were actually there.

As time passes, even those who never knew the ruler begin to worship the statue. The skill of the artist makes the image look even more impressive, and the people, amazed by its beauty, begin to treat it as a god.

People are deceived into thinking that something man-made has divine power.

But they did not stop there. They drifted even further from the truth,

justifying their foolishness and calling their evil actions "peace."

They went so far as to sacrifice their own children, take part in secret rituals, and engage in wild, uncontrolled celebrations.

They lost all respect for life and marriage, falling into betrayal, adultery, and dishonesty.

The world became filled with violence, murder, theft, deception, corruption, unfaithfulness, chaos, and lies.

People lost their sense of right and wrong. They forgot kindness, had no gratitude, and defiled themselves. Their relationships were ruined by cheating and uncontrolled desires.

The worship of false gods—idols that should never have existed—is the root of all evil, its cause, and its ultimate result.

Those who take part in such worship lose control of themselves. They spread false messages, commit injustice, and have no problem lying under oath.

Since they believe in lifeless statues, they make false promises without fear of consequences.

But their own words and actions will bring punishment upon them.

By worshiping idols, they have insulted God, disrespected His holiness, and led others astray.

It is not the fake gods they swear by that will condemn them,

but their own sins.

God's justice will not fail—He will hold the wicked accountable for everything they have done.

Chapter 15

You, our God, are full of kindness and truth. You are patient and merciful, carefully watching over everything.

Even when we make mistakes, we are still yours because we recognize your authority. Knowing we belong to you gives us the strength to turn away from sin.

To truly understand you is what it means to be righteous, and knowing your power is the key to eternal life.

We have not been fooled by the tricks of people or by the meaningless work of artists who create statues and decorate them with bright colors.

These images may attract the attention of those who lack wisdom, but they are nothing more than lifeless objects with no breath or spirit.

Those who make, desire, and worship such things are chasing after emptiness and will become just as worthless as the idols they honor.

A potter takes soft clay and skillfully shapes it into useful objects.

From the same material, he makes items for both important and ordinary uses, deciding their purpose based on his own choice.

But sometimes, he takes that same clay and creates an idol that has no purpose at all.

This man, who was recently formed from the dust of the earth, will soon return to it when his short life comes to an end. His soul, which was only borrowed, will be taken back.

Yet instead of thinking about how brief his life is, he works anxiously—not because he values his time on earth, but because he wants to compete with goldsmiths, silversmiths, and other craftsmen, showing off his skills in making false gods.

His heart is as worthless as ashes. His hopes are weaker than dust, and his life has even less meaning than the clay he shapes.

This is because he does not know his Creator—the one who gave him life, filled him with a soul, and breathed His spirit into him.

Instead, he treats life as a game and his days as nothing more than an opportunity to gain wealth. He tells himself, "I must become rich no matter what, even if I have to do wrong."

Such a man fully understands his sin. He takes fragile clay to make both everyday items and false gods, yet he does not see how pointless his actions are.

Even more foolish and hopeless are those who are enemies of your people—those who have mistreated them.

They bow down to the idols of nations, treating them as gods, even though these statues cannot see, breathe, hear, touch, or walk.

These idols were made by human hands, created by people who themselves rely on the breath of life. No person can make a god.

The craftsmen who build these idols are more valuable than the statues they worship because at least they are alive, while the idols have never had life at all.

Even worse, these people worship the lowest and most meaningless creatures. Compared to other living beings, these are the most foolish and senseless.

They have no beauty that would make anyone admire them. They do not deserve praise and have never received any blessing from God.

Chapter 16

Because of their actions, they were rightfully punished by the very creatures they worshiped, suffering from swarms of insects and vermin.

But in contrast, you blessed your people. You provided them with quail, a rich and satisfying food to meet their hunger.

This happened so that their enemies, desperate for food, would be disgusted by the swarms of pests you sent, losing even the desire to eat. Meanwhile, your people, though they experienced a brief moment of need, were given fine and nourishing food.

It was fair for the oppressors to endure constant suffering, while your people only needed to see the punishment of their enemies.

Even when your people were attacked by wild animals and deadly snakes, your anger did not last long.

You sent these challenges as a warning and gave them a sign of salvation to remind them of your laws.

Those who looked at the sign were not saved by the object itself but by you, the one who rescues all.

Through this, you showed their enemies that only you have the power to save people from danger.

Their enemies were bitten to death by swarms of insects, with no cure for their suffering, because they deserved their punishment.

But your people were protected from the poison of deadly snakes. Your mercy healed them and kept them safe from harm.

They were bitten only as a reminder of your commandments, but you quickly healed them to teach them about your kindness and to prevent them from being ungrateful.

It wasn't herbs or medicine that cured them, but your word, O Lord, which heals all things.

You alone have control over life and death. You lead people to the brink of the grave and bring them back again.

Even when the wicked take life through their evil actions, they cannot return a lost soul or set a captive spirit free.

No one can escape your power.

The ungodly, who refused to recognize you, were struck by your mighty hand. You punished them with strange storms, hail, endless rain, and consuming fire.

In a miraculous way, fire burned even hotter in water—something that should have put it out—proving that creation itself fights to protect the righteous.

At times, the fire was held back so it wouldn't destroy the creatures sent to punish the wicked, allowing them to see that they were under your judgment.

At other times, the fire burned fiercely, even in water, to destroy the crops of an unrighteous land.

But for your people, you provided bread from heaven, food that required no work to prepare. This special bread, which tasted perfect to everyone, satisfied all cravings.

Your kindness was clear in how the bread adjusted to each person's preference, showing your deep care for your children.

Even snow and ice resisted the fire and did not melt, proving that fire destroyed the wicked's crops while burning through hail and flashing through the rain.

But when the fire was needed to help the righteous, it softened its strength and acted with control.

Creation itself, serving you as its Maker, uses its power to punish the wicked while showing kindness to those who trust in you.

At that time, creation changed to serve your people, revealing your endless mercy and care.

This taught your beloved children that it is not food from the earth that truly sustains life, but your word, which protects those who rely on you.

What the fire did not burn melted away with just a gentle ray of sunlight,

Teaching your people to wake early to thank you and to pray as a new day begins.

But the hope of the ungrateful fades like frost in the morning sun, vanishing like water that flows aimlessly and serves no purpose.

Chapter 17

Your judgments are deep and beyond full understanding, and because of this, those without discipline strayed far from the truth.

When lawless people thought they could take control of a holy nation, they found themselves trapped in total darkness. Bound by chains of endless night, they remained hidden inside their homes, cut off from your eternal care.

They thought their secret sins would never be discovered, but instead, they were caught in a heavy cloud of forgetfulness. Fear gripped them, and they were tormented by terrifying visions.

Even the dark places where they tried to hide couldn't protect them from their overwhelming panic. They were surrounded by strange and eerie sounds, and frightening shadows with stern faces appeared before them.

No fire could break through the thick darkness, and not even the brightest stars could light their way.

Instead, a faint, ghostly glow filled them with dread. They became more afraid of the terrifying things their minds imagined than the actual shadows they could see but refused to face.

The magic they once used to mock others was useless now. Their proud claims of wisdom turned into shame and embarrassment.

Those who once bragged about calming troubled minds were now consumed by ridiculous fears.

Even when there was no real danger, they panicked at the sound of insects crawling or the quiet hissing of snakes.

They were frozen in fear, trembling, too scared to even look around, even though the air surrounded them completely.

Wickedness is always cowardly, haunted by its own guilty conscience. The weight of guilt brings fear, making people imagine the worst possible things.

Fear is nothing but the loss of clear thinking.

When reason is thrown away, ignorance takes its place, making the suffering even worse.

As the night covered them like a heavy shadow from the grave, they all suffered the same restless sleep.

They were haunted by terrifying visions, and sudden, unexpected fear took control of them.

No matter what they were doing—standing, lying down, or working—they felt trapped, as if invisible chains were holding them back.

It didn't matter if they were farmers, shepherds, or workers in the wilderness; all of them were consumed by the same overwhelming terror, bound by the heavy chains of darkness.

Even the smallest sounds—wind whispering, birds chirping, water rushing down violently, or stones crashing—filled them with fear.

The quick movements of unseen animals, the growls of wild creatures, or echoes bouncing off mountain caves froze them in place.

While the rest of the world enjoyed bright, clear light and carried on with their daily lives,

They were covered in deep, crushing darkness. It felt like the shadow of eternal night, a warning of what was to come. They felt trapped, as if they were heavier and more weighed down than the darkness itself.

Chapter 18

For your faithful people, you provided a bright and guiding light. Meanwhile, their enemies could hear their voices but couldn't see them. Even though these enemies had harmed them before, they chose not to do so now. Instead, they felt relief that they had also suffered and began to regret the harm they had caused. Some even sought forgiveness.

You gave your people a pillar of fire to lead them on their unknown journey. It acted like a gentle sun during their time of exile, bringing them hope. But the Egyptians, who had imprisoned your children, deserved to be left in the darkness, just as they had tried to keep your people from bringing the light of your law to the world.

After they plotted to destroy the children of the faithful, you saved one abandoned child to expose their guilt. In return, you took their own children and swept away their mighty army in a great flood.

You warned our ancestors about that night ahead of time so they could hold onto your promises and find comfort in their faith. They waited with hope—trusting that the righteous would be saved and that their enemies would be punished. While you brought judgment on their oppressors, you honored your people and brought them closer to you.

Holy children of faithful families made their sacrifices in secret. Together, they entered into the sacred covenant, sharing both the blessings and dangers that came with it. Their ancestors led them in songs of praise. At the same time, cries of grief echoed from their enemies, mourning the children they had lost.

Both slaves and rulers suffered the same punishment, as did the rich and the poor. No one was spared, and countless bodies lay unburied. The living couldn't even bury their dead because, in an instant, their most beloved children had been taken from them.

Even though they had relied on magic and refused to believe in the truth, they were finally forced to admit that the people of God were truly His chosen ones after their firstborn were struck down.

As the earth lay in deep silence and the night reached its darkest point, your powerful word came down from heaven, from your royal throne. Like a fierce warrior, it entered the land that was doomed for destruction, carrying out your sharp command. Death spread everywhere, from the highest places to the lowest.

Terror swept through them. Their dreams filled them with fear, and panic gripped their hearts. They fell to the ground, barely alive, and suddenly realized why they were dying. Their dreams had warned them of what was coming, so they understood exactly why they were suffering.

Even the righteous were touched by death, and many were lost in the wilderness. But your anger did not last long. A pure and faithful man stepped forward to plead for the people. Using prayer and sacred incense as his weapons, he stood between life and death, stopping the disaster and proving his loyalty to you.

He calmed your wrath, not by using physical strength or weapons, but through his words. He reminded you of the promises and oaths you had made to their ancestors, and in doing so, he held back the destroyer. As the dead fell in great numbers, he stepped in and stopped the destruction before it could reach the living.

The robe he wore represented the entire world, and the history of his people was engraved in four rows of precious stones. Your majesty rested upon the crown he wore on his head.

Chapter 19

God's fierce anger struck the wicked without holding back until the very end because He already knew what they would do. Even after letting His people go and urging them to leave, He knew they would soon change their minds and chase after them.

While they were still grieving and crying over their dead, they made another foolish choice. They decided to pursue the very people they had begged to leave and forced out of their land, treating them like runaway slaves.

Their own punishment led them toward their downfall, making them forget the suffering they had already endured. This happened so they could fully experience the justice they deserved and face the consequences of their actions.

Meanwhile, your people traveled on an incredible path, while their enemies met a strange and terrible fate.

All of creation adjusted to follow your commands and protect your people. A cloud covered the camp, providing shelter, and dry land appeared where there had once been water. The Red Sea opened up into a clear road, and a grassy plain rose from the wild waves. Protected by your hand, your people crossed safely, watching these amazing miracles unfold.

They moved with ease, like horses running through an open field, and leapt like joyful lambs, singing praises to you, O Lord, their Savior.

They remembered the miracles of their journey: how the land, instead of producing livestock, became overrun with swarms of lice, and how the river, instead of fish, was filled with countless frogs.

Later, when they craved rich and satisfying food, they saw a new kind of bird appear. To meet their needs, quails rose from the sea, providing them with nourishment and comfort.

But sinners were not punished without warning. The rumbling thunder had already given them a sign of what was coming. They were justly punished for their cruelty, for they had treated strangers with extreme harshness.

While some simply refuse to welcome outsiders, the Egyptians took it much further—they enslaved the very people who had once helped them. At first, they welcomed their guests with feasts, but later, they forced them into brutal labor, even though they had once lived side by side.

They were also struck with blindness, just like others had been at the doorstep of a righteous man. Trapped in total darkness, they desperately searched for a way out but couldn't even find their own doors.

Just as the strings of a harp create different sounds, the forces of nature changed in amazing ways.

Land animals turned into sea creatures, while those that once swam moved onto dry land. Fire burned fiercely even within water, and water changed its nature to put out flames.

Yet the fire did not harm the creatures walking through it, nor did it melt the delicate grains of heavenly food, which could dissolve so easily.

In every way, O Lord, you showed your power to your people. You honored them, never turning away, and stayed by their side in every place and at every moment.

Psalms of Solomon

This collection of eighteen war songs is a rare treasure from an ancient Semitic writer. Although the original manuscript was lost over time, Greek translations have survived, and a Syriac version was later discovered. In 1909, Dr. Rendel Harris translated this Syriac version into English, allowing people to read these powerful songs once again.

These songs were written around the mid-First Century B.C. Their main focus is on the actions of Pompey in Palestine and his eventual death in Egypt in 48 B.C. The historical background connects these verses to real events from that time.

These psalms were highly valued in the early Church and were shared widely among believers. They appear in different ancient texts and historical records from the first few centuries of Christianity. However, for reasons that remain unclear, they eventually stopped being used and were forgotten. After many centuries, they have been rediscovered and made available once more.

Besides their historical importance, these songs also stand out for their poetic beauty. Their words flow with the rhythm of battle, like the sound of trumpets, stirring the emotions of the reader. The psalms paint a vivid picture of ancient history, as if written by someone who witnessed the events firsthand.

The verses describe Pompey as he comes from the West, leaving destruction behind him. He uses battering rams to tear down city walls, defiles the temple altar, and is ultimately killed in Egypt after a violent and ruthless campaign. In these songs, the "righteous" seem to represent the Pharisees, while the "sinners" may symbolize the Sadducees. These psalms are more than just poetry—they tell the dramatic story of a people struggling to survive in the midst of chaos and war.

Psalm 1

I cried out to the Lord when I was overwhelmed with trouble, calling on God when sinners rose against me. Suddenly, the sounds of war surrounded me, but He heard me because I tried to live righteously.

In my heart, I believed I was righteous, for I had been blessed with success and many children. Their wealth and status spread far and wide, and their glory seemed to reach the heavens.

But in their pride, they believed they could never fall. As they grew richer, they became arrogant. They stopped bringing offerings to God and hid their sins from me, keeping them secret.

Their wrongdoing became worse than those who came before them, and they dishonored the Lord's sacred place with their corruption.

Psalm 2

A psalm about Solomon and Jerusalem.

When the wicked became proud, they used battering rams to break down the strong walls, and You, Lord, did not stop them. Foreign nations invaded Your altar, stepping on it with arrogance. The people of Jerusalem had already defiled Your holy place, dishonoring Your sacred gifts with their sinful actions.

Because of this, You said, "Send them far from Me; I take no joy in them." The beauty of Jerusalem no longer pleased You, and her honor was completely destroyed. Her sons and daughters were taken away as captives, wearing the shame of slavery among the nations.

You judged them for their sins, handing them over to their enemies. You turned away from them and showed no mercy, letting both young and old suffer because they refused to listen to Your commands. Heaven was filled with sorrow, and the earth trembled, for no people on earth had done such terrible things.

The whole world will come to understand Your righteous judgments, O God. They humiliated the sons of Jerusalem, treating them with cruelty, while strangers defiled her before the sun even rose. They openly embraced evil and mocked Your law. The daughters of Jerusalem were disgraced, losing their purity in confusion and sin.

My soul aches, and my heart is heavy because of all this. But still, I will praise You, O God, with a heart that seeks righteousness, for Your judgments are always just. You have repaid the wicked for their sins, exposing their wrongdoing to prove Your justice. Their memory has been wiped from the earth, for You, O God, are a fair and righteous judge.

The nations laughed at Jerusalem, crushed her underfoot, and stripped away her beauty. She traded her fine clothes for rags, and her crown was replaced with a rope. The glorious headdress You gave her was thrown aside, and her splendor was covered in shame.

Seeing this, I cried out to You, Lord, and pleaded:

"Hasn't Jerusalem suffered enough under Your judgment? You have allowed the nations to mock and destroy her without mercy. Put an end to their fury before they wipe her out completely. You alone, Lord, can bring her back from this ruin."

Psalms Of Salomon 2–4

Punish them in Your anger, O Lord, for they did not act out of devotion to You but out of selfish greed. They unleashed their fury on us through violence and theft. Do not wait, O God—make them suffer the consequences of their own actions. Expose their arrogance and bring down the prideful enemy.

It did not take long before God revealed their foolishness. In the mountains of Egypt, he was struck down, becoming more despised than the lowest among both land and sea. His body was tossed on the waves in disgrace, with no one to bury him, for God had rejected him in shame.

He forgot that he was just a man and never considered what would come after this life. He proudly declared, "I will rule over the earth and the sea," but he did not realize that God alone is great and powerful. The Lord is the true King of heaven, the One who judges rulers and authorities.

God lifts up the humble and brings down the arrogant, casting them into eternal disgrace because they refused to acknowledge Him. Now, let all the leaders of the earth see the Lord's justice, for He is a righteous King who rules over everything under the heavens.

Praise the Lord, all who honor Him with wisdom, for He shows mercy to those who fear Him and live righteously. He separates the righteous from the wicked, punishing sinners for their actions while showing kindness to the faithful.

The Lord saves those who trust in Him from the shame brought by the wicked and repays sinners for the harm they have done to His people.

The Lord is good to those who call on Him with faith, treating His followers with love and keeping them safe in His strength.

Blessed is the Lord forever, worshiped and praised by His servants.

Psalm 3

Why do you sleep, my soul, and forget to praise the Lord? Sing a new song to God, for He is worthy of all honor. Wake up and play music for Him with all your heart, for a joyful song comes from a heart that loves Him.

The righteous always remember the Lord, giving thanks and trusting in His justice. They do not resist His discipline because they know He is always good. Even when they face struggles, they do not blame Him but wait patiently for His help. They keep their eyes on Him, knowing He is their salvation.

Their righteousness comes from their Savior, and sin does not take hold in their homes. They carefully examine their lives, making sure to remove anything that leads them away from God. Through fasting and humbling themselves, they seek forgiveness for sins they did not realize they committed. The Lord purifies the hearts of those who are devoted to Him and blesses their homes.

But sinners curse their lives, their birth, and even the pain their mothers went through to bring them into the world. They continue in their sin, going deeper into evil without any hope of turning back. Their destruction will last forever, and they will be forgotten by the righteous.

This is the destiny of sinners, but those who fear the Lord will have eternal life. The light of the Lord will shine on them, and they will live with Him forever, never to be separated from His presence.

Psalm 4

Why do you, someone who disrespects the holy, sit among the faithful while your heart is far from the Lord?

You anger the God of Israel with your sinful actions.

You speak proudly, acting as if you are better than everyone else.

You judge harshly but are quick to condemn others for their sins.

PSALMS OF SALOMON 4–5

You strike first as if you are passionate for righteousness, but you are guilty of many sins and selfish pleasures.

Your eyes wander to every woman without care, and your words are full of lies when you make promises.

At night, when no one is watching, you sin as if you cannot be seen. You use secret signals to tempt women and enter homes pretending to be innocent.

May God remove such hypocrites from among His faithful people—those who live in corruption and selfishness.

May God expose their actions, showing their lies and shame. Let the faithful praise God's justice when sinners are removed from the righteous.

A people-pleaser twists the law for his own gain, setting his sights on the home of a good man, like a serpent waiting to destroy wisdom with clever words.

He lies to get what he wants, leaving innocent people helpless.

He ruins families with his sinful actions, deceiving others while thinking no one will see or judge him.

Filled with wickedness, he goes from house to house, spreading chaos with his words.

Like the grave, he is never satisfied. O Lord, let him face disgrace before You.

May his days be filled with suffering, and his nights with restless sorrow.

May his work fail, and his home be left empty.

Let him grow old in loneliness, without children, until the end of his life.

May his body be left for wild animals to devour, and may the bones of sinners lie in disgrace under the sun.

May ravens pluck out the eyes of those who destroy families, chasing after their own desires.

They have forgotten You, O God, and have no fear of You.

They have angered and provoked You.

Remove them from the earth, for they have deceived the innocent with false kindness.

Blessed are those who fear the Lord with pure hearts.

The Lord will rescue them from liars and sinners and protect them from the traps of the wicked.

May God remove the arrogant who do wrong, for He is a great and powerful judge who rules with justice.

Let Your mercy, O Lord, be upon all who love You.

Psalm 5

A psalm of Solomon.

O Lord God, I will gladly praise Your name among those who know Your just and fair judgments.

You are kind and full of mercy, a safe place for the poor. When I call out to You, please do not ignore me.

No one can take anything from a strong man unless You allow it, Lord. Everything, including people and what they have, is measured by You. No one can receive more than what You have decided.

When we are in trouble, we call on You, O God, because You are our protector, and Your judgments are always right.

You do not forget the cries of those who suffer or the needs of the poor.

Keep us safe and lead us, O Lord, for Your name is our strong refuge, and Your righteousness lasts forever.

Psalms Of Salomon 5–8

You will not ignore our prayers, for You are our God, faithful and true. Do not let Your hand be too heavy on us, or in our suffering, we may turn to sin. If You bring us back to You, we will not wander far but will return with open and willing hearts.

If I am hungry, I will cry out to You, O God, and You will provide for me. You take care of the birds in the sky and the fish in the sea. You send rain to dry lands, making grass grow for all living things. You feed wild animals and provide for every creature that depends on You.

You sustain kings, rulers, and entire nations, O Lord. Who else can the poor and needy turn to except You, their God? You hear them, for You are kind and forgiving. You bring joy to the humble and show mercy to all who seek You.

People often give with hesitation, delaying their kindness for another day. Even when they help without complaint, true generosity is rare. But Your blessings, Lord, are rich and overflowing, given freely to those who put their trust in You.

Your mercy covers the whole earth, O Lord, and Your kindness reaches all of creation. Blessed is the one whom You remember and provide for, giving them exactly what they need. Too much leads to sin, but true happiness comes from having just enough, along with righteousness.

This is where Your favor is found—a life filled with goodness and justice. May those who fear the Lord rejoice in His kindness, and may Your love rest upon Israel in Your kingdom.

Blessed is the glory of the Lord, for He is our King.

Psalm 6

In Hope. A Psalm of Solomon.

Blessed is the one whose heart is always ready to call on the name of the Lord. When they remember Him, salvation is near. The Lord guides their steps and protects the work of their hands.

They will not be troubled by bad dreams or afraid when crossing rivers or facing stormy seas. When they wake up, they praise the name of the Lord. With a strong and faithful heart, they sing songs of worship to their God.

They pray to the Lord for their family, and He listens to all who respect and honor Him. He fulfills the desires of those who place their hope in Him.

Blessed is the Lord, who shows mercy to those who truly love Him.

Psalm 7

A Psalm of Solomon. A Prayer for Restoration.

Do not leave us, O God, or our enemies will rise against us. You have already rejected them—do not let them trample the land You have given to Your people.

Correct us, O Lord, as You see fit, but do not hand us over to other nations. Even if You allow death to come, it will only happen by Your command, for You are merciful and will not stay angry forever.

As long as Your name is with us, we will find mercy, and no nation will be able to defeat us. You are our shield and protector. When we call on You, You hear us.

Your love for Israel never ends. You will never abandon Your people. We remain under Your care, shaped by Your correction and guided by Your wisdom.

When the time comes for You to rescue us, You will show mercy to the house of Jacob, keeping the promises You made.

Psalm 8

A Psalm of Solomon. A Song of Victory.

I heard the sounds of trouble—the noise of war.

Trumpets blasted, warning of violence and destruction.

The cries of many people roared like a powerful wind, like a storm sweeping through the land, burning everything in its path.

In my heart, I wondered, "Where will God bring justice for all this?"

Psalms Of Salomon 8–9

I heard a cry from Jerusalem, the city of God's holy temple. The news crushed my spirit—I trembled, my knees felt weak, and my heart filled with fear. My whole body shook as if my bones were breaking. I thought to myself, "Surely, they will turn back to God and follow His ways."

I reflected on God's judgments, which have been in place since the creation of heaven and earth, and I recognized the fairness of His eternal decisions. God revealed their sins in the open, in the bright light of day. All the earth witnessed His righteous justice.

Yet in secret places, deep in the shadows, they committed terrible sins, breaking God's law without shame. Sons slept with their mothers, fathers with their daughters. Men broke sacred vows, committing adultery with their neighbors' wives. They swore oaths to protect each other in their wickedness.

They stole from God's sanctuary as if there was no one to stop them. They defiled His altar with impurity, treating holy sacrifices as worthless, even desecrating them with blood. They committed every kind of sin, surpassing even the nations in their corruption.

In response, God sent confusion upon them. He gave them over to their sins like drunkards lost in their own wickedness. From distant lands, He brought a powerful enemy who waged war against Jerusalem and its people.

The leaders of the city welcomed this enemy with joy, saying, "Come in peace; we welcome you to our land." They made the roads smooth for his arrival, opened Jerusalem's gates, and decorated the city as if preparing for a celebration.

But he did not come in peace. He entered like a conqueror, walking through the streets with pride and power. He seized Jerusalem's towers and broke through its walls, for God had allowed it while the people continued in their disobedience.

He slaughtered their rulers and silenced their wise men. The blood of Jerusalem flowed like polluted water. He captured their sons and daughters—children born in sin—and took them into captivity.

Still, they continued in their wicked ways, just as their ancestors had done. They desecrated Jerusalem and defiled everything that had been set apart for God's name. Yet through all this, God's judgment remained just, for He is holy and righteous.

The faithful, innocent like lambs, stood in the midst of these punishments. Blessed is the Lord, who judges the earth with fairness. "We have seen Your justice, O God. We have witnessed Your truth with our own eyes."

We honor Your name, lifted high forever, for You are the God of righteousness. You discipline Israel with justice. Show us mercy once again, O God. Gather the scattered people of Israel with kindness and love, for Your faithfulness never fails.

Though we have been stubborn, You are the One who corrects us. Do not leave us, O God, or the nations will destroy us as if we had no Savior. You have been our God from the beginning, and You are still our hope, O Lord.

We will not turn away from You, for Your judgments are fair and merciful. Your goodness remains with us and our children forever.

O Lord, our Savior, we will never be shaken again.

Blessed and praised is the Lord for His righteous judgments, spoken by the mouths of the faithful.

And blessed is Israel, forever secure in the Lord.

Psalm 9

A Psalm of Solomon. A Call to Repentance.

When Israel was taken away to a foreign land and turned from the Lord who had saved them, they lost the inheritance He had given them. They were forced to leave, separated from the land of their ancestors.

In exile, they remembered God's correction, feeling the heavy weight of their sins. They mourned their distance from His promises and cried out for Him to restore them.

But even in their punishment, the Lord remained merciful, for He is a faithful and righteous God.

Psalms Of Salomon 9–11

The people of Israel were scattered among the nations, fulfilling God's word, so that Your justice, O Lord, would be proven right in the face of our sins. You are a fair judge over all the earth, and Your judgments will never change.

No act of injustice is hidden from You. You see everything Your faithful servants do, O Lord. No one can hide from Your knowledge, O God.

Each person chooses their own path—whether to follow righteousness or to walk in sin. In Your fairness, You hold everyone accountable and judge them by their actions.

Those who live righteously store up life in Your presence, but those who live in wickedness bring destruction upon themselves. Your judgments are always right, applying to every person and every family.

Who will receive Your kindness, O God, if not those who call on You with honest hearts? You wash away sin for those who admit their wrongs and seek forgiveness. Shame weighs heavy on us, O Lord, and we bow our heads in regret for all we have done.

Who else will You forgive but those who humbly confess their sins? You bless the righteous and do not turn away from them because of past mistakes. You show kindness even to sinners who repent and return to You.

Now, You are our God, and we are the people You have loved and chosen. Look upon us with mercy, O God of Israel, for we belong to You. Do not take Your kindness away from us, or our enemies will defeat us.

You chose the descendants of Abraham above all nations and placed Your name upon us, O Lord. You will not abandon us forever. You made a promise to our ancestors on our behalf, and we trust that You will restore us when we turn back to You.

The Lord's mercy lasts forever over the house of Israel, keeping us through every generation.

Psalm 10

A Hymn of Solomon.

Blessed is the one whom the Lord remembers and corrects, guiding them away from the path of sin. His discipline helps cleanse them so that sin does not take over their life.

Those who humbly accept correction will be made pure, for the Lord is kind to those who endure His teaching. He keeps the righteous on the right path and does not let them go astray.

The Lord's mercy is with those who truly love Him. He remembers His servants with compassion, for His truth is written in His everlasting law. His covenant stands as a testimony to His ways and His care for humanity.

Our God is righteous and faithful in all His judgments, forever. Let Israel lift its voice in praise and rejoice in the name of the Lord.

The faithful will speak of His goodness among the people, and the Lord will show mercy to the poor, bringing joy to the hearts of Israel.

For God is kind and full of mercy, and His love lasts for all time. Let the people of Israel praise His name, for His salvation brings eternal joy to His people.

Psalm 11

A Psalm of Solomon. A Call to Hope.

Blow the trumpet in Zion, calling the holy ones together. Announce the good news in Jerusalem, for the God of Israel has shown His mercy and come to His people.

Stand on the heights, O Jerusalem, and see your children returning, gathered once more by the Lord.

From the east and the west, they come back to You, O Lord, rejoicing in their God.

From the north and the farthest islands, God has brought them home, uniting them through His mercy and power.

PSALMS OF SALOMON 11–14

The Lord has made the high mountains level and the hills smooth, clearing a path for His people.

Psalm 13

The forests provided shade as they passed, and God made fragrant trees grow along their path. This was so that Israel could walk through and see the glorious presence of their God.

Jerusalem, dress yourself in glory and put on the robe of holiness, for God has spoken everlasting blessings over Israel.

May the Lord keep His promises to Israel and Jerusalem. May He lift up His people by the power of His glorious name, for His mercy and love will always remain with Israel.

Psalm 12

A Psalm of Solomon.
   A Prayer Against the Words of the Wicked.

O Lord, save me from the wicked and lawless,
   from those who speak lies and spread slander.

The words of the corrupt are twisted and destructive,
   like a fire that burns through a city, leaving it in ruins.

He spreads falsehoods to destroy homes,
   tearing down joy and bringing chaos with his lies.

He stirs up conflict and turns people against each other,
   using his deceitful words to bring division into peaceful
   places.

O God, protect the innocent from the harm of these evildoers.
Scatter the bones of the slanderers far away,
   far from those who honor You.

Let every lying tongue be silenced in the fire of judgment,
   far from the faithful who love You.

Watch over those who seek peace and justice,
   and guide those who build harmony in their homes.

The Lord's salvation is upon His servant Israel forever.
Let the sinners be removed from His presence,
and let the faithful receive His promises,
for His mercy endures for those who remain strong in faith.

The Lord's right hand has shielded me,
protecting us from destruction.

His mighty power saved us from the sword,
from hunger, and from death that waits for the wicked.

Fierce beasts rose up against them,
tearing their flesh with sharp teeth,
crushing their bones with mighty jaws.

But the Lord rescued us from every danger.

The faithful feel sorrow over their own sins,
fearing they might be caught in the fate of the wicked.
But the judgment upon sinners is terrible,
and it will not come near the righteous.
The discipline of the faithful is different from
the punishment of sinners.
God corrects His people with care,
so the wicked cannot mock or take joy in their struggles.

He rebukes the righteous as a loving father corrects his child,
guiding them as one would a firstborn.

The Lord spares His faithful ones,
cleansing their wrongs through His discipline.

The righteous will live forever,
    but sinners will face destruction,
    and their names will be forgotten.

The Lord's mercy is endless for those who follow Him,
    and His compassion is upon those who fear Him.

God is faithful to those who love Him sincerely,
    to those who accept His correction with patience.

He blesses those who walk in righteousness,
    following His commands that lead to life.

The faithful will live by His words forever,
    like trees in His garden, bearing fruit that never fades.

Their roots are deep and strong,
    never to be uprooted as long as the heavens endure.

The Lord cares for His faithful ones,
    and His promises stand as their unshakable foundation.

All who walk in His ways will thrive in His light,
    living by the law of life He has given to His people.

Psalms Of Salomon 14–16

God's chosen people, Israel, are His special inheritance, the ones He loves. But this is not true for those who sin and reject His laws. They chase after temporary pleasures and embrace wrongdoing. They focus on their own desires and forget about God and His ways.

God sees everything about every person, even the hidden thoughts of the heart before they form. Because of this, sinners will inherit darkness, destruction, and eternal separation from Him. On the day when God shows mercy and favor to the righteous, sinners will not stand, for their own actions have sealed their fate.

But those who love the Lord and follow His ways will receive eternal life, and their joy will never end.

When I was struggling and felt hopeless, I called on the name of the Lord. I placed my trust in the God of Jacob, and He saved me.

For You, O God, are a safe place and a source of hope for the humble and the poor. Who is truly strong, O Lord, except the one who trusts in You completely? And what power does anyone have except in praising Your name?

With songs of joy and hearts full of gratitude, we lift up our voices to You. These praises come from a faithful and righteous heart, the first and best offerings of thankfulness to You. Those who live this way will not be shaken by evil. The fire of judgment will not touch them.

When Your anger falls upon sinners, O Lord, everything they own will be destroyed. But Your protection is upon the righteous, keeping them safe. Famine, war, and death will not come near them, for trouble will flee from them as if chased away.

Sinners, however, will not escape Your judgment, Lord. They will be overtaken by destruction, for they have been marked for ruin. Their inheritance is darkness, suffering, and despair. The wrong they have done will follow them even after death.

Their wealth and possessions will not last, and their children will not inherit anything from them, for their sins will destroy everything they leave behind.

On the day of the Lord's judgment, when God brings justice to the earth, sinners will be wiped out forever. They will face the full weight of His righteous anger.

But those who fear the Lord, who respect and love Him, will receive mercy on that day. They will be saved by His kindness and grace.

However, the unrepentant and rebellious sinners will be destroyed forever, never to rise again.

Psalm 16

A Hymn of Solomon. A Prayer for Help.

When my soul drifted away and fell into deep sleep, I stumbled, lost like those who live without God. For a moment, I felt myself slipping toward death, nearing the gates of the grave alongside sinners.

But even when I felt distant from the God of Israel, His endless mercy saved me. He reached out, waking me like a rider prods a horse to move, stirring me to return to Him. He has always been my Savior and Protector, rescuing me when I was weak.

I will praise You, O God, with a thankful heart, for You lifted me up and gave me salvation. You did not let me be counted among those destined for destruction.

Do not take Your mercy from me, O God. Let me always remember You, even to my last breath. Rule over my heart, Lord, and protect me from sin and every temptation that leads people astray.

Do not let me be deceived by the beauty of someone who disrespects Your law or by anything that tempts me to sin. Guide the work of my hands so that I may serve You, and lead my steps so I always walk in Your ways.

Keep my mouth and lips pure, so that only words of truth come from me. Remove all anger and reckless wrath from my heart, so they do not lead me into sin. Help me not to complain or lose faith when I go through hardship.

Lord, keep me strong in faith and truth. Let Your guidance and mercy be the light that leads me, keeping me close to You always.

Psalms Of Salomon 16–17

When I sin, You correct me to bring me back to the right path, Lord. Your discipline has a purpose—it is how You restore me.

Fill my heart with strength and joy, for when You support me, everything You provide is enough. Without Your help, who could handle the weight of discipline, especially during times of struggle and hardship?

When a person is corrected while caught in sin, Your testing often comes through challenges in life and the struggles of poverty. But if the righteous stay strong through these trials, they will find Your kindness and mercy, O Lord.

Psalm 17

A Psalm of Solomon. A Song About the King.

O Lord, You are our King forever. In You, O God, we find our confidence and strength.

Life on earth is short, measured by the days we live and the hope we place in You. But we will trust in You completely, our Savior. Your power lasts forever, full of mercy, and Your kingdom rules with justice over all nations for all time.

You, O Lord, chose David to be king over Israel and promised him that his descendants would always have a place before You. But because of our sins, enemies rose against us. They attacked and drove us out, though You never gave them that right. They took what did not belong to them and refused to honor Your holy name.

In their arrogance, they built great palaces, thinking they could change what You had set in place. They disrespected David's throne, acting as if they could undo Your will. But You, O God, will bring them down. You will erase their descendants from the earth when You raise up a new ruler, one unlike them. You will punish them for their sins, making sure they face the consequences of their actions.

You showed them no mercy. You wiped out their descendants so none could escape Your judgment. O Lord, You are faithful and just in all Your judgments across the earth.

The wicked destroyed our land, leaving it barren and empty. They killed both the young and the old, showing no mercy—not even to children. In Your anger, You drove them to the west. The rulers of the land were mocked and not spared. The enemy, though an outsider, was proud and had no fear of You, O God.

In Jerusalem, he behaved as the nations do in their own fortified cities. But even among those who were supposed to be faithful, no one showed mercy or upheld the truth. Those who once loved gathering to worship You fled like birds leaving their nests. They wandered in the wilderness to escape evil, and their survival was a sign to those who watched from afar.

The wicked scattered them across the earth. The heavens held back the rain, and the underground springs stopped flowing. The highest mountains became dry because righteousness and justice were nowhere to be found. From kings to common people, all had fallen into sin. The rulers broke Your law, the judges disobeyed, and the people followed in their wickedness.

O Lord, look upon Your people and rise up for them. Send their king, the son of David, at the time You have chosen. Let him rule over Israel, Your servant. Give him strength to break the power of corrupt rulers, cleanse Jerusalem from those who destroy her, and lead with wisdom and justice. Let him drive sinners out of the land You have given to Your people.

Let him crush the pride of the wicked like clay in a potter's hands and destroy their wealth with an iron rod.

Let him defeat sinful nations with the words of his mouth. At his command, may his enemies scatter, and sinners tremble with guilt even in their own hearts. He will gather a holy people and lead them in righteousness.

Psalms Of Salomon 17–18

He will rule over the tribes of God's people, the ones made holy by the Lord. He will not allow injustice to remain among them, and no one who does evil will live among them. He will know them well, understanding that they are all God's children.

He will give them their inheritance, dividing the land among the tribes. No outsider will live among them anymore. With wisdom and fairness, he will judge both his own people and the nations.

He will bring the nations under his rule, placing them under his authority. He will bring glory to the Lord across the earth, making Jerusalem holy again and restoring its purity. People from all over the world will come to see his greatness. They will bring gifts and return the scattered sons of Jerusalem. They will witness the shining glory that God has placed upon His city.

He will be a just and righteous king, taught by God Himself. During his reign, there will be no injustice among his people, for all will live in holiness, and he will be the Lord's chosen leader. He will not rely on horses, warriors, or weapons. He will not gather gold and silver for war or trust in a large army to win battles.

Instead, the Lord will be his King and his source of strength, as he places all his hope in God. He will show mercy to every nation that respects him. With the power of his words, he will bring justice to the earth and bless God's people with wisdom and joy. He will live free from sin so that he can lead his people, correct rulers, and remove the wicked with the truth of his words.

He will not waver, always depending on his God. The Lord will fill him with strength through the Holy Spirit, giving him wisdom, understanding, guidance, and righteousness. God's blessing will be with him in everything he does. His trust will be firmly in the Lord, and no one will be able to defeat him.

His actions will be great, and his reverence for God will make him strong. He will lead God's people with fairness and care, making sure that no one is left behind or forgotten. He will guide them with justice, ensuring that no one is treated unfairly or oppressed.

This is the greatness of the king of Israel—the one God has chosen and prepared to rule His people and lead them with discipline and wisdom. His words will be more valuable than the finest gold, more precious than the purest treasures. Among the people, he will judge with wisdom, and his words will be honored as holy among God's chosen ones.

Blessed are those who will live in that time and witness the goodness of Israel, as God restores His people and unites the tribes once again.

May the Lord quickly show mercy to Israel and free His people from those who have defiled them.

The Lord Himself will always be our King, reigning forever.

Psalm 18

God, Your kindness lasts forever in everything You have made. You pour out Your goodness on Israel like a precious gift. When You look at them with love, no one is left in need. You always listen to the cries of the poor who trust in You.

Your justice reaches across the whole earth, but it is full of mercy. Your love stays strong for the descendants of Abraham, the children of Israel, whom You have chosen. Like a caring parent, You guide us with discipline, treating us like a beloved firstborn child, correcting us and leading us away from foolishness.

May God make Israel pure, preparing them for the time of His kindness. May He bless them richly and cover them with His grace.

Psalms Of Salomon 18

On the day God chooses, when He sends His anointed one, blessed are those who will see it. Lucky are those who will witness God's goodness and the amazing things He will do for future generations. Under the leadership and guidance of God's chosen one, people will honor and respect their Lord, living with wisdom, justice, and strength.

This anointed leader will teach everyone to do what is right and help them grow in their respect for God. He will lead them to stand firmly before the Lord, creating a generation devoted to holiness during a time of God's mercy.

Pause and reflect with the sound of music. Our God is great, lifted high above all things. He set the stars and planets in motion, marking the seasons and keeping track of time. These lights in the sky have never strayed from the paths He gave them.

From the moment God created them, they have followed His will. For countless generations, they have remained steady in their course, only changing direction when He commands, passing His instructions through His faithful servants.

Odes of Solomon

These songs are among the most beautiful expressions of peace and joy in the world today. However, their origins, the time they were written, and the exact meaning behind many of their verses remain a literary mystery.

The songs have survived in a single ancient manuscript written in Syriac, which seems to be a translation from the original Greek. Scholars have debated their history for years, and one of the most accepted theories is that they were created by newly baptized Christians in the First Century.

What sets these songs apart is that they do not reference historical events. They do not draw from the Old Testament or the Gospels, making their inspiration feel fresh and original. They echo the words of Aristides, who once described early Christians as "a new people with something Divine within them." The power and depth of these songs are comparable to the most moving passages of Scripture.

These remarkable and mysterious odes were translated for us by J. Rendel Harris, a well-respected scholar and Honorary Fellow of Clare College, Cambridge. He describes them as works of extraordinary beauty and deep spiritual meaning, stating, "The only thing people seem to agree on is that the Odes are uniquely beautiful and hold great spiritual value."

Ode 1

The Lord rests on my head like a crown, and He will never leave me.

The crown of truth has been placed on me, and it has made Your branches grow within me.

It is not a dry or lifeless crown that does not bloom.

You live upon me, and through You, I have flourished.

Your fruits are abundant and whole, filled with the salvation that comes from You.

Ode 2

[There is no extant copy of Ode 2]

Ode 3

I am wrapped in the love of the Lord.

His people are with Him, and I rely on them, just as He loves me.

I would not have known how to love the Lord if He had not first shown me His endless love.

Only someone who has been loved can truly understand love.

I love the One who loves me, and wherever He finds rest, I will be there too.

I will never feel like an outsider, because the Lord Most High is merciful and has no jealousy.

I am united with Him, for love has brought us together. Since I love the Son, I will also be called a child of God.

Anyone who is connected to the Eternal One will also share in eternal life.

Whoever finds joy in the Source of Life will also be filled with life.

This is the Spirit of the Lord, which is true and never deceives. It teaches people to understand His ways.

Be wise, gain understanding, and open your heart to His truth.

Hallelujah.

Ode 4

No one can change or take away Your holy place, O my God.

No one has power over it because You designed Your sanctuary long before creating sacred places.

What is ancient and holy cannot be changed by anything lesser. Lord, You have given Your heart to those who believe in You.

You are never still, and You always bring life and growth.

Just one moment of Your faithfulness is greater than all days and years combined.

Who can receive Your grace and then be rejected?

Your seal is known, and all Your creation recognizes it.

Your heavenly hosts carry it, and Your chosen archangels are clothed in it.

You have invited us to be with You, not because You need us, but because we always need You.

Pour out Your gentle rain upon us and open Your overflowing springs, filling us with all we need.

You never regret what You have promised, and nothing You say will ever change.

You knew the outcome from the very beginning.

What You have given, You have given freely, never to take it back.

Everything was clear and perfectly planned by You from the start.

Lord, You are the Creator of all things.

Hallelujah.

Ode 5

I praise You, Lord, because I love You.

O Most High, do not leave me, for You are my hope.

You have given me Your grace freely; may I live by it always.

My enemies may come after me, but do not let them find me.

Cover their eyes in darkness and surround them with thick shadows.

Let them have no light to guide them, so they cannot capture me.

Let their own plans trap them, so whatever they have plotted comes back on them.

They made their schemes, but they were never meant to succeed.

They prepared to harm me, but in the end, they were powerless.

My trust is in the Lord, and I will not be afraid.

Because the Lord is my salvation, I have nothing to fear.

He is like a crown upon my head, holding me steady.

Even if everything around me shakes, I will stand firm.

Even if all I see fades away, I will not be lost.

For the Lord is with me, and I am with Him.

Hallelujah.

Ode 6

Just as the wind moves through a harp and makes the strings play,

The Spirit of the Lord moves through me, and I speak with His love.

He removes everything that does not belong, for all things belong to the Lord.

This has been true from the beginning and will remain true forever.

Nothing can stand against Him, and nothing can rise above Him.

The Lord has spread His wisdom and wants His gifts to be known through His grace.

He gave us His praise for the sake of His name, and our spirits glorify His Holy Spirit.

A small stream began to flow and became a mighty, wide river, sweeping away everything in its path and leading to His Temple.

No walls built by people could stop it, nor could those skilled in controlling water hold it back.

It spread across the earth, filling everything in its way.

Then all who were thirsty drank deeply, and their thirst was satisfied.

For this drink was given by the Most High.

Blessed are those who serve this water, for they have been entrusted with His life-giving gift.

They refreshed dry lips and awakened weary hearts.

Even those close to death were revived by them.

They strengthened weak bodies and restored what had been broken.

They gave energy to the weary and brought light to fading eyes.

Everyone recognized them as belonging to the Lord, for they lived by His eternal, life-giving water.

Hallelujah.

Ode 7

Just as anger rises against evil, so does joy overflow for the Beloved, bringing blessings without limits.

My joy comes from the Lord, and my path leads to Him. This journey is beautiful.

I have a Helper—the Lord—who has revealed Himself to me with kindness and humility, making His greatness feel close.

He became like me so that I could receive Him. He took on my form so that I could welcome Him.

When I saw Him, I was not afraid, because He was full of grace toward me.

He made Himself like me so I could understand Him and see that He is near.

The Father of knowledge is the source of wisdom.

He who created wisdom is greater than anything He has made.

Before I even existed, He knew me and what I would do once I was born.

Because of this, He poured out His endless grace, allowing me to seek Him and receive the gift of His sacrifice.

He is perfect, unchanging, and the Creator of all worlds.

He has revealed Himself to those who belong to Him so they would recognize their Maker and understand that they did not create themselves.

He has opened the way to knowledge, making it wide, clear, and complete.

He has marked it with His light, stretching from the beginning to the end.

Everything serves Him, and the Son brings Him joy.

Through His salvation, He will claim all things as His own, and the Most High will be revealed to His holy ones.

They will proclaim His coming to those who sing of the Lord, so they may go out to meet Him with joy and music.

The prophets will go before Him, standing in His presence.

They will praise Him with love, for He is near and sees everything.

Hatred will disappear, and jealousy will be drowned.

Ignorance will be wiped away, for the knowledge of the Lord will fill the earth.

Let those who sing lift up the name of the Lord Most High and bring their songs of praise.

Let their hearts shine like daylight and their voices reflect the beauty of the Lord.

Let no one remain silent or without understanding.

For He gave every living being a voice to praise Him and declare His glory.

Let all speak of His power and share the goodness of His grace.

Hallelujah.

Ode 8

Open your hearts to the joy of the Lord, and let your love flow from within to your words.

Live a holy life, bearing good fruit for the Lord, and speak with wisdom in His light.

Rise up and stand tall, you who were once brought low.

You who were silent, speak now, for your mouth has been opened.

You who were once rejected, be lifted up, for your righteousness has been raised high.

The Lord's right hand is with you, and He will be your Helper.

Peace has been prepared for you, even before any battle you may face.

Listen to the word of truth and receive the wisdom of the Most High.

Your body may not understand what I am about to say, nor can your clothing reveal what I am about to show you.

Hold on to my mystery, you who are protected by it; hold on to my faith, you who are kept by it.

Understand my wisdom, you who truly know me; love me deeply, you who love.

I do not turn away from my own, for I know them.

Even before they existed, I saw them and placed my mark upon them.

I shaped their being and prepared my own nourishment for them, so they could drink from my holiness and live.

I take joy in them and am not ashamed of them.

They are my creation, made from my thoughts and purpose.

Who can stand against what I have made? Who can resist my will?

I created mind and heart, and they belong to me. I have placed my chosen ones in my right hand.

My righteousness goes before them, and they will never lose my name, for it remains with them.

Pray, grow, and remain in the love of the Lord.

You are loved in the Beloved, kept safe in the One who lives, and saved by the One who was saved.

You will remain unshaken for all generations because of the name of your Father.

Hallelujah.

Ode 9

Listen carefully, and I will speak to you.

Give yourself to me, so I may also give myself to you.

This is the word of the Lord and His plan—the holy purpose He has for His Messiah.

In the Lord's will, you find life; His purpose leads to eternal life, and His perfection never fades.

Be strengthened in God the Father, accept His plan, and stand firm, redeemed by His grace.

I bring you a message of peace, His holy ones, so that none who hear will fall in battle.

Those who know Him will not be lost, and those who receive Him will never feel ashamed.

Truth is an everlasting crown—blessed are those who wear it.

It is more precious than any jewel, for many battles have been fought over it.

But righteousness has claimed it and now offers it to you.

Wear this crown as a sign of your covenant with the Lord, and all who overcome will be written in His book.

For His book is the reward of victory, and it sees you before it, longing for you to be saved.

Hallelujah.

Ode 10

The Lord has guided my words with His truth and opened my heart with His light.

He has placed His eternal life within me and allowed me to share the blessings of His peace.

To help those who seek Him find new life and to lead those in bondage into freedom.

I found strength and courage, and I took hold of the world. What was once captivity became mine for the glory of the Most High, my God and Father.

Those who had been scattered were gathered together, but my love for them did not make me unclean, because they honored me in high places.

His light touched their hearts, and they followed my path, finding salvation. They became my people forever.

Hallelujah.

Ode 11

My heart was made clean, and its beauty bloomed. Then grace grew within me, and I produced good fruits for the Lord.

The Most High purified me with His Holy Spirit, opening my heart to Him and filling it with His love.

His cleansing became my salvation, and I walked in His path, in His peace, and in the way of truth.

From the beginning to the end, He gave me understanding.

He placed me on the rock of truth, making me strong where He had set me.

His refreshing waters touched my lips, flowing freely from the fountain of the Lord.

I drank deeply and was filled with joy from the living water that never runs dry.

This joy did not lead me to ignorance, but it made me turn away from worthless things.

I left behind empty pursuits and turned to the Most High, my God, gaining the riches of His blessings.

I rejected the foolishness of the world, threw it aside, and left it behind me.

The Lord gave me new garments and covered me in His light.

From above, He gave me eternal rest, and I became like a land full of life, blooming with joy.

The Lord shines upon me like the sun over the earth.

My eyes were opened, and my face was refreshed with His dew.

My breath was filled with the sweet fragrance of the Lord.

He brought me into His Paradise,
    where the treasures of His joy are stored.
I saw trees blooming and bearing fruit,
    Their crowns growing naturally,

Their branches reaching upward,
and their fruit shining brightly.
Their roots came from an everlasting land,
Watered by a river of joy,
Flowing through the land of eternal life.

Then I worshiped the Lord, amazed by His greatness.

I said, "Blessed are those, O Lord, who are planted in Your land and have a place in Your Paradise.

They grow like the trees You have planted, leaving darkness behind and stepping into light."

Look at all Your faithful workers—they are beautiful, doing what is right and turning away from evil to follow Your goodness.

The scent of every tree in Your land is changed, becoming sweet and pure.

Everything reflects You, Lord. Blessed are those who care for Your waters, and may Your faithful servants be remembered forever.

There is plenty of room in Your Paradise, and nothing is empty or barren—everything is full of fruit.

Glory to You, O God, the joy of Paradise forever.

Hallelujah.

Ode 12

He has filled me with words of truth so that I can speak about Him.

Just like water flows, truth flows from my mouth, and my lips share the good things He has done.

He has given me great knowledge because the Lord's words are true, and His light brings understanding.

The Most High has given Him to His people—
> Those who explain His beauty,
> Those who tell of His greatness,
> Those who admit His plans,
> Those who share His thoughts,
> And those who teach about His works.

His words are beyond description, and just as He speaks with wisdom, He also moves with speed and sharpness, never slowing down.

He never falls but always stands firm, and no one can fully understand where He comes from or how He works.

Just as He does His work, He also brings hope, for He is the light that brings new ideas.

Through Him, generations spoke to one another, and even those who were silent found their voices.

Love and fairness came from Him, and people spoke to each other with kindness.

His words inspired them, and they came to know their Creator because they were united.

The Most High spoke to them, and His message spread because of Him.

The Word lives within people, and His truth is love.

Blessed are those who, through Him, understand all things and know the Lord in His truth.

Hallelujah.

Ode 13

Look! The Lord reflects who we are. Open your eyes and see yourself in Him.

Learn what you truly look like, and then praise His Spirit.

Wipe away anything that hides your true self, love His holiness, and make it a part of you.

Then, you will always remain pure with Him.

Hallelujah.

Ode 14

My eyes are always looking to You, Lord, just as a child looks to their father.

My joy and my heart belong to You.

Please don't turn away Your mercy, Lord, and never take Your kindness from me.

Reach out Your hand to me always, my Lord, and guide me to the end according to Your will.

Let me be pleasing to You because of Your greatness, and save me from evil for the sake of Your name.

Let Your gentleness stay with me, Lord, along with the blessings of Your love.

Teach me the songs of Your truth so I can grow and bear good fruit in You.

Open my heart to the music of Your Holy Spirit, so I can praise You with every note, Lord.

Show me Your mercy in abundance, and answer our prayers quickly.

For You are all we need.

Hallelujah.

Ode 15

Just as people rejoice when they see the sunrise, my joy comes from the Lord.

He is my Sun, and His light has lifted me up, driving away all darkness from my face.

Through Him, I have been given sight and have seen His holy day.

He has given me ears to hear His truth.

I have gained understanding and found great joy in Him.

I turned away from the wrong path, went toward Him, and received His abundant salvation.

Because of His kindness, He blessed me, and in His great beauty, He shaped me.

Through His name, I have put on eternal life, and by His grace, I have left behind all that fades away.

Death has disappeared before me, and the grave has lost its power because of His word.

Eternal life has begun in the Lord's kingdom, and it has been revealed to His faithful people, given freely to all who trust in Him.

Hallelujah.

Ode 16

Just as a farmer's work is with the plow, and a sailor's work is steering the ship, my work is singing to the Lord through His songs.

My passion and purpose are found in His hymns because His love has filled my heart, and He has placed His words on my lips.

The Lord is my greatest love, so I will sing to Him.

His praises give me strength, and I trust in Him completely.

When I open my mouth, His Spirit will speak through me, sharing the glory and beauty of the Lord—

The work of His hands, the detail of His creation,

The depth of His mercy, and the power of His Word.

For the Word of the Lord reveals what is unseen and makes His thoughts known.

Our eyes witness His creation, and our ears hear His wisdom.

He stretched out the land and placed the waters in the sea.

He spread out the sky and set the stars in place.

He shaped all of creation, set everything in motion, and then rested from His work.

All things follow their paths and fulfill their purpose, never stopping or failing.

Even the heavenly beings obey His Word.

The sun holds the light, and the night holds the darkness.

He made the sun to shine by day, and the night to bring darkness across the land.

Together, they reflect the beauty of God's design.

Nothing exists outside of the Lord, for He was here before anything began.

Everything was created by His Word and His wisdom.

Praise and honor to His name.

Hallelujah.

Ode 17

Then my God placed a crown on me, and it was full of life.

My Lord declared me righteous, for my salvation will never fade away.

I have been freed from empty pursuits, and I am no longer condemned.

He broke my chains with His own hands, gave me a new identity, and saved me as I walked with Him.

The truth guided my thoughts, and I followed it without losing my way.

Everyone who saw me was amazed, as if I were a stranger to them.

The One who truly knows me and lifts me up is the Most High, perfect in all things.

Through His kindness, He honored me and lifted my understanding to the highest truth.

From there, He showed me the path to follow, and I opened doors that had once been shut.

I broke through iron bars, for the chains that once held me had melted away.

Nothing was closed off to me, because He made me a way for all things to open.

I went to those who were still trapped so I could set them free, making sure no one remained in bondage.

I shared my knowledge freely, and through my love, I brought new life.

I planted my truth in people's hearts and changed them from within.

Then they received my blessing and truly lived, coming together and finding salvation.

They became part of me, and I became their leader.

Glory to You, our Head, O Lord Messiah.

Hallelujah.

Ode 18

My heart was lifted and filled with the love of the Most High so that I could praise Him with all that I am.

He gave me strength so I would not fall away from His power.

Sickness left my body, and I stood strong for the Lord because His kingdom will never be shaken.

Lord, for the sake of those in need, do not take Your Word away from me.

And do not hold back Your goodness because of what others do.

Let light never be defeated by darkness, and let truth never be chased away by lies.

Let Your mighty hand bring salvation to victory, gathering people from everywhere and protecting those who suffer.

You are my God—there is no falsehood or death in You; only perfection is in Your will.

You do not know what is empty and meaningless, because such things do not belong to You.

You are never mistaken, and mistakes cannot exist in You.

Foolishness appeared like dust in the wind, like foam on the sea.

Some people thought it was something great, but they became like it—empty and weak.

But those who understood saw the truth and did not let their minds be corrupted.

They stayed close to the thoughts of the Most High and saw the foolishness of those who had lost their way.

Then they spoke truth with the breath that the Most High had placed within them.

Praise and great honor to His name.

Hallelujah.

Ode 19

A cup of milk was given to me, and I drank it, tasting the sweetness of the Lord's kindness.

The Son is the cup, the Father is the one who provides the milk, and the Holy Spirit is the one who gathers it.

His blessings were overflowing, and it was meant to be shared, not wasted.

The Holy Spirit poured out this gift, blending the richness of the Father's love.

She gave it to the world without them realizing, and those who received it were made whole by His power.

The Virgin's womb took it in, and she conceived and gave birth.

She became a mother, filled with deep mercy.

She gave birth without pain because it was all part of a greater purpose.

She needed no midwife, for He Himself brought life through her.

With strength and great desire, she delivered Him, fulfilling what was promised by God's power.

She embraced Him with love, protected Him with kindness, and declared His glory.

Hallelujah.

Ode 20

I am a priest of the Lord, and I serve Him faithfully.

To Him, I offer the sacrifice of His own wisdom.

For His wisdom is not like the world's, not like the flesh, nor like those who worship in a worldly way.

The Lord desires offerings of righteousness, a pure heart, and truthful words.

Give yourself to Him with honesty, and do not let your kindness be a burden to others, nor treat others unfairly.

Do not take advantage of a stranger, for they are like you. Do not deceive your neighbor or take away what they need.

Instead, clothe yourself in the Lord's grace and enter His paradise. Take from His tree and make for yourself a crown.

Wear it with joy, rest in His presence, and be at peace.

His glory will go before you, and you will receive His kindness and grace. You will be anointed in truth and sing praises to His holiness.

Praise and honor to His name.

Hallelujah.

Ode 21

I lifted my arms high because of the Lord's kindness.

He broke my chains and set me free. My Helper lifted me up with His mercy and salvation.

I left behind the darkness and stepped into the light.

He made me whole, and my body was free from pain, sickness, or suffering.

The Lord's wisdom guided me, and His presence was always with me.

He lifted me into the light, and I stood before Him.

I stayed close to Him, always praising and thanking Him.

He filled my heart so much that His praise overflowed from my mouth and onto my lips.

Then my face shined with joy, celebrating the Lord and His goodness.

Hallelujah.

Ode 22

He brought me down from above and lifted me up from below.

He gathers what is in between and hands it over to me.

He scattered my enemies and those who stood against me.

He gave me the power to break chains so I could set others free.

Through me, He defeated the seven-headed dragon and placed me at its roots so I could destroy its offspring.

You were always with me, guiding me, and Your name surrounded me everywhere I went.

Your mighty hand wiped out its poisonous evil and cleared the path for those who believe in You.

You called people out of their graves and separated them from the dead.

You took dry bones and covered them with flesh.

But they remained still, so You filled them with the breath of life.

Your ways and Your presence never change. You allowed the world to decay so that everything could be restored and made new.

The foundation of all things is built upon You, the solid rock. Upon it, You have built Your kingdom, a home for those who are holy.

Hallelujah.

Ode 23

Joy belongs to those who are holy. Who else can truly receive it but them?

Grace is given to those chosen by God. And who can accept it except those who have trusted in it from the very beginning?

Love is for those whom God has set apart. And who can embrace it but those who have carried it in their hearts from the start?

Walk in the wisdom of the Lord, and you will experience His grace in abundance—both for His glory and the fullness of His truth.

His wisdom was like a letter sent down from above,

Shot like an arrow from a powerful bow.

Many hands reached out, trying to grab it, hoping to take hold and read it.

But it slipped through their fingers, and they feared both the letter and the seal upon it.

They could not break the seal, for the power behind it was greater than them.

Still, some followed after it, wanting to know where it would land, who would read it, and who would hear its message.

Then a great wheel caught the letter and carried it forward.

With it came a sign of the kingdom and God's plan.

Everything that stood in its way was cleared out and removed.

It silenced many enemies and made a way where there was none.

It crossed over rivers, tore down forests, and created a clear path.

The head bowed down to the feet, for the wheel moved beneath them, carrying everything along with it.

The letter carried a command, and all the nations gathered together.

At its head was the One who was revealed—the Son of Truth, sent from the Most High Father.

He took possession of all things, and the plans of those who opposed Him came to nothing.

Those who tried to deceive others became weak and fled, and those who persecuted Him vanished.

Then the letter became a great book, completely written by the hand of God.

The name of the Father was upon it, along with the Son and the Holy Spirit, to reign forever and ever.

Hallelujah.

Ode 24

The dove fluttered above the head of our Lord Messiah because He was her leader.

She sang over Him, and her voice was heard.

The people were afraid, and strangers were unsettled.

The bird took flight, and every small creature hid away.

Deep places opened and closed, as if searching for the Lord like a mother about to give birth.

But He was not given to them as food, for He did not belong to them.

Instead, the deep places were sealed by the Lord, and they disappeared along with their old ways of thinking.

They had struggled from the beginning, but their struggle led to life.

Yet those who were lacking perished because they could not hold on to the truth.

The Lord destroyed the plans of those who did not have truth in them.

They lacked wisdom, even though they thought highly of themselves.

So they were cast aside, for they did not have the truth.

But the Lord made His way clear and poured out His grace for all to see.

And those who understood recognized His holiness.

Hallelujah.

Ode 25

You set me free from my chains, and I ran to You, my God.

You are the hand that saves me and my Helper in times of need.

You stopped those who rose against me, and they disappeared.

Because Your presence was with me, and Your grace saved me.

But many looked down on me and rejected me, treating me like something worthless.

Yet You gave me strength and helped me.

You placed a lamp on both my right and left, filling me with light so that no darkness remained in me.

Your Spirit covered me, and I left behind my old self.

Your mighty hand lifted me up and took away my sickness.

I became strong in Your truth and holy in Your righteousness.

All my enemies feared me, and I belonged fully to the Lord.

Your kindness made me right with You, and Your peace lasts forever.

Hallelujah.

Ode 26

I lifted my voice in praise to the Lord because I belong to Him.

I will sing His holy song because my heart is with Him.

His harp is in my hands, and His songs of peace will never be silenced.

With all my heart, I will call to Him, praising and honoring Him with everything in me.

From the East to the West, His name is praised.

From the South to the North, He is thanked.

From the highest peaks to the farthest ends, His greatness is seen.

Who can write the songs of the Lord, or who can truly understand them?

Who can prepare himself for eternal life and save himself?

Who can reach the Most High and make Him speak?

Who can explain the wonders of the Lord? Even if the one who tries is gone, what he spoke of will remain.

It is enough to understand and be fulfilled, for those who sing for the Lord stand in perfect peace—

Like a river flowing from a powerful spring, bringing refreshment to those who seek it.

Hallelujah.

Ode 27

I lifted my hands and honored my Lord,

For stretching out my hands is a sign of Him.

And my outstretched arms form the shape of the cross.

Hallelujah.

Ode 28

The Spirit surrounds my heart like a mother dove covering her young, feeding them with care.

My heart is always renewed and filled with joy, like a baby leaping in its mother's womb.

I trusted in Him, and so I found peace, because the One I trust is always faithful.

He has blessed me greatly, and I am with Him.

No weapon can separate me from Him—not a dagger, not a sword.

I am prepared before trouble comes, standing on His side, which never dies.

Eternal life has embraced me and filled me with love.

The Spirit within me comes from that life, and it cannot die, because it is life itself.

People were shocked when they saw me suffering.

They thought I was defeated, like someone who was lost forever.

But what seemed like my downfall became my salvation.

They rejected me because I had no jealousy in my heart.

I was hated for constantly doing good.

They attacked me like wild dogs, foolishly turning against the One who cared for them.

Their thoughts were twisted, and their hearts were full of confusion.

But I carried water in my right hand, and I met their bitterness with kindness.

I did not fall because I was not like them, and I was not born from the same place as they were.

They wanted to destroy me, but they couldn't, because I existed before their time, and their plans against me were useless.

Even those who tried to erase the memory of the One before them failed.

For the wisdom of the Most High cannot be controlled, and His ways are greater than all understanding.

Hallelujah.

Ode 29

The Lord is my hope, and I will never be ashamed of trusting in Him.

He created me to bring Him praise, and in His kindness, He has blessed me.

By His mercy, He lifted me up, and through His great honor, He raised me high.

He brought me out of the depths of death and saved me from its grasp.

He helped me defeat my enemies and made me right through His grace.

I put my faith in the Lord's Messiah and knew that He is the Lord.

He showed me His sign and guided me with His light.

He gave me His power so I could stand against the plans of the wicked and humble the strength of the powerful.

By His Word, I fought the battle and won the victory through His might.

The Lord crushed my enemy with His Word, scattering him like dust in the wind.

So I give praise to the Most High, for He has honored His servant and the son of His faithful one.

Hallelujah.

Ode 30

Come and take water from the Lord's living fountain—it has been opened for you.

All who are thirsty, come and drink. Rest beside the Lord's fountain.

Its water is pure, sparkling, and always refreshing.

It is sweeter than honey, and no honeycomb can compare.

For it flows from the Lord's lips and comes straight from His heart.

It came without limits, unseen, and many did not recognize it until it was placed before them.

Blessed are those who drink from it and are renewed.

Hallelujah.

Ode 31

Deep valleys disappeared before the Lord, and darkness faded when He appeared.

Lies collapsed and were destroyed by Him, and arrogance had no place because the truth of the Lord overcame it.

He opened His mouth and spoke words of grace and joy, singing a new song to His name.

Then He lifted His voice to the Most High and presented to Him those who became His children through Him.

His face shined with righteousness, just as His Holy Father had intended.

Come, all who are suffering, and receive joy.

Take hold of His grace and accept the gift of eternal life.

They judged me even though I had done no wrong.

They took what was mine, even though they had no right to it.

But I stayed calm and silent, refusing to be shaken by them.

I stood firm, like a strong rock that is struck again and again by crashing waves but does not move.

I endured their cruelty with humility so that I could save my people and guide them.

I did this to keep the promises made to the ancestors, for I was sent to bring salvation to their descendants.

Hallelujah.

Ode 32

Joy fills the hearts of those who are blessed, and light comes from the One who lives within them.

The Word of truth exists by itself,

For it is strengthened by the Holy Power of the Most High and will never be shaken.

Hallelujah.

Ode 33

But grace moved quickly and cast out the Deceiver, coming down to reject him.

He brought destruction before him and ruined everything he had done.

He stood on the highest peak and shouted from one end of the earth to the other.

He gathered all who followed him, because he did not appear as the Evil One.

But the pure and faithful one stood firm, calling out and saying:

"O sons of men, turn back! And you, daughters, come to me.

Leave the path of the Deceiver and follow me instead.

I will come into your lives, rescue you from destruction, and teach you the ways of truth.

Do not let yourselves be ruined or lost.

Listen to me and be saved, for I bring you the grace of God.

Through me, you will be saved and find blessing. I am your judge.

Those who follow me will not be falsely accused but will live forever in the new world.

My chosen ones walk with me, and I will show my ways to those who seek me. I will give them my name as a promise."

Hallelujah.

Ode 34

There is no struggle for those with a pure heart, and no obstacle for those who think rightly.

A clear mind is not shaken by chaos.

When someone is surrounded by goodness, they remain whole and at peace.

What is above reflects what is below.

For everything comes from above, and what seems to come from below only appears real to those who lack understanding.

Grace has been revealed to save you. Believe, live, and be saved.

Hallelujah.

Ode 35

The gentle rain of the Lord covered me with peace, and a cloud of calmness rose above my head.

It stayed with me, protecting me at all times, and became my salvation.

People around me were troubled and afraid, and from them came anger and judgment.

But I remained at peace in the Lord's presence—He was my shelter, stronger than any foundation.

He carried me like a mother carries her child and nourished me with the Lord's kindness.

His favor filled my life, and I found rest in His perfection.

I lifted my hands and turned my heart toward the Most High, and He saved me.

Hallelujah.

Ode 36

I rested in the Spirit of the Lord, and She lifted me up to heaven.

She set me on my feet in the Lord's high place, before His greatness and glory, where I praised Him with songs.

The Spirit brought me into the presence of the Lord, and because I was the Son of Man, I was called the Light, the Son of God.

I was honored above all the honored ones and made greater than the great ones.

For just as the Most High is great, He made me great, and just as He is always new, He renewed me.

He anointed me with His perfection, and I became one of those close to Him.

My words poured out like refreshing dew, and my heart overflowed with righteousness.

I walked in peace and was strengthened by the Spirit of God's care.

Hallelujah.

Ode 37

I lifted my hands to the Lord and raised my voice to the Most High.

I spoke from deep within my heart, and He heard me when my words reached Him.

His Word came to me, bringing the reward for my efforts.

And He gave me rest through His grace.

Hallelujah.

Ode 38

I entered the light of Truth as if riding in a chariot, and the Truth guided me forward.

It led me safely over deep valleys and dangerous cliffs, protecting me from harm.

It became my place of safety and set me on the path to eternal life.

He walked with me, gave me rest, and kept me from going the wrong way because He is and always will be the Truth.

I was never in danger because I stayed close to Him, and I never lost my way because I followed His voice.

For deception runs from Him and never crosses His path.

But Truth moves straight ahead, showing me what I did not understand—

Revealing the lies that poison the mind and the pain that disguises itself as pleasure.

I saw the corruption of the Deceiver, how he dressed up falsehood to look beautiful, pretending to be a bridegroom with a bride.

I asked the Truth, "Who are they?" And He answered, "This is the Deceiver and the Lie."

"They try to imitate the Beloved and His Bride, leading the world astray and filling it with corruption."

"They invite many to their false wedding feast and give them wine that clouds their minds."

"They make people forget their wisdom and throw away their knowledge, replacing it with foolishness."

"Then they abandon them, leaving them lost, wandering like people without direction."

"They do not seek understanding because they have none."

But I was made wise so that I would not fall into the hands of the Deceivers, and I rejoiced because the Truth was with me.

I was made strong, I lived, and I was saved, for the Lord's hand had laid my foundation.

He planted me, setting my roots deep, watering and blessing me so that my fruit would last forever.

I grew strong, spreading out and thriving.

And the Lord alone was glorified—

In His planting, His care, and His blessing.

In the beauty of His work and the wisdom of His plan.

Hallelujah.

Ode 39

The powerful rivers of the Lord rush forward, sweeping away those who reject Him.

They block their paths, destroy their crossings,

Pull them under, and ruin them completely.

These waters move faster than lightning, even more swiftly than the wind.

But those who cross with faith will not be harmed.

Those who walk on them with trust will not be shaken.

Because the Lord's mark is on these waters, and His sign is the path for those who cross in His name.

So take on the name of the Most High and know Him, and you will pass through safely, for the rivers will obey you.

The Lord has made a way across them with His Word—He walked on them and crossed on foot.

His footsteps stayed firm on the waters and did not disappear; they are like a strong bridge built on truth.

Waves rose high on both sides, but the steps of our Lord Messiah remained steady.

They were never washed away or destroyed.

And this path has been prepared for those who follow after Him—those who stay true to His faith and worship His name.

Hallelujah.

Ode 40

Just as honey drips from a honeycomb and milk flows from a mother to her child, so my hope flows to You, O my God.

Like a fountain pouring out water, my heart overflows with praise for the Lord, and my lips speak His glory.

His songs make my tongue sweet, and His music fills my whole being.

My face shines with joy in His presence, my spirit celebrates His love, and my soul glows in Him.

Those who are afraid can put their trust in Him, for He brings sure salvation.

He gives the gift of eternal life, and those who receive it will never be destroyed.

Hallelujah.

Ode 41

Let all of God's children praise Him, and let us accept the truth of His faith.

His people are known by Him, so let us sing with joy because of His love.

We have life through the Lord's grace, and we receive it through His Messiah.

A great light has shined on us, and the One who shares His glory with us is truly wonderful.

So let us all come together in the name of the Lord and honor Him for His goodness.

Let our faces shine in His light, and may our hearts reflect on His love, day and night.

Let us celebrate with the joy of the Lord.

People who see me will be amazed because I am different from them.

For the Father of Truth remembered me—the One who has known me from the beginning.

His riches brought me into being, formed from the thoughts of His heart.

His Word is with us wherever we go—our Savior, who gives life and never rejects us.

He humbled Himself but was lifted up because of His righteousness.

The Son of the Most High appeared, reflecting the perfection of His Father.

Light shined from the Word, which existed before time began.

The Messiah is the one true Savior. He was known before the world was created so that He could bring eternal life through the power of His name.

A new song of praise belongs to the Lord from those who love Him.

Hallelujah.

Ode 42

I lifted my hands and reached out to my Lord, for stretching out my hands is a sign of Him.

My arms formed the shape of the upright cross, the same cross that was raised for the Righteous One.

I became invisible to those who never truly knew me, for I will not show myself to those who do not belong to me.

But I will be with those who love me.

All who persecuted me have perished. They searched for me, those who spoke against me, because I am alive.

Then I rose and stood with my people, speaking through their voices.

For they have turned away from their persecutors, and I covered them with the love that binds them to me.

Like a bridegroom holding his bride, so is my love upon those who know me.

And just as a bridal chamber is prepared for the wedding, my love surrounds those who believe in me.

Though I was rejected, I did not truly fall, and though they thought I was gone, I did not perish.

The grave saw me and was shattered, and death released me along with many others.

I became bitterness to death, sinking deep into its depths.

But it could not hold me—its power was broken, and it let go of my hands and feet because it could not withstand my presence.

Among the dead, I created a gathering of the living. I spoke to them with words full of life, so that my message would not be wasted.

Those who had died ran toward me, crying out:

"Son of God, have mercy on us!

Show us Your kindness and set us free from the chains of darkness.

Open the door so we may come to You, for now we see that death has no power over You.

Save us as well, for You are our Savior!"

I heard their cries and held their faith in my heart.

Then I placed my name upon their heads, for they were now free, and they belong to me.

Hallelujah.

Testaments of the Twelve Patriarchs
(Selected Excerpts)

Introduction

The twelve books in this collection are biographies written between 107 and 137 B.C. They show how a skilled Pharisee used the names of some of history's greatest figures to share important lessons. These figures, known as the Twelve Patriarchs, were highly respected leaders of their time.

Each Patriarch tells his life story in these writings. As they lay on their deathbeds, they gathered their children, grandchildren, and great-grandchildren to share their wisdom. They spoke with complete honesty, hoping to guide their families toward a righteous life. If a Patriarch had made mistakes, he openly admitted them and warned his descendants not to follow the same path. If he had lived a good and faithful life, he explained how his choices brought him blessings.

Beyond their personal stories, these writings provide an incredible glimpse into the early belief in a coming Messiah, more than a century before Christ. Another important aspect of this collection is its moral teachings. As Dr. R.H. Charles noted in his study of ancient Jewish writings, the ethical lessons in these texts had a lasting impact. They shaped not only the thinking and language of the New Testament writers but, at times, even the teachings of Christ Himself. These moral lessons go beyond those in the Old Testament while still remaining true to its message, creating a connection between Old and New Testament values.

The influence of these writings on the New Testament is especially clear in the Sermon on the Mount, which reflects their ideas and even uses some of their phrases. The Apostle Paul also seems to have been deeply influenced by these writings, using their ideas and language so often that it is possible he carried a copy with him on his journeys.

This collection of writings is unique because it combines a simple, direct style with deep spiritual meaning. These texts played a key role in shaping the moral and religious ideas that later influenced the Bible.

Testament of Reuben

The Firstborn Son of Jacob and Leah.

Chapter I.

Reuben, the oldest son of Jacob and Leah, was a man who had learned many lessons in life. He wanted to share his wisdom about avoiding temptation, especially the dangers of giving in to desire. He taught how young people can easily make mistakes and how they can protect themselves from falling into sin.

This is the record of Reuben's final words, including the advice he gave to his children before he died at the age of 125.

Two years after his brother Joseph passed away, Reuben became very sick. When his sons, grandsons, and great-grandsons heard about his illness, they gathered to see him one last time. Knowing his time was short, Reuben called them together and said, "My children, my life is coming to an end, and I will soon go the way of my ancestors."

His brothers Judah, Gad, and Asher also came to visit him. Reuben asked them, "Help me sit up, so I can share something I have kept in my heart for a long time. My time to leave this world is near."

After they helped him up, he kissed them and said, "Listen carefully, my brothers, and you, my children, pay attention to my words."

"I call upon God as my witness today—do not follow the sins of youth. Do not fall into temptation as I once did, when I defiled my father Jacob's bed. Because of my sin, God punished me with a painful illness that lasted seven months. If my father Jacob had not prayed for me, I would not have survived."

"I was thirty years old when I committed this terrible sin before the Lord. For seven months, I was seriously ill, barely clinging to life. Afterward, I repented deeply. For seven years, I fasted and prayed, refusing wine, strong drinks, and anything enjoyable. I did not eat meat or allow myself any pleasure, because my sin was so great— something never seen before in Israel."

Reuben continued, "Now, my children, let me tell you what I learned during my time of repentance about the seven spirits of deception that mislead people."

"There are seven spirits that try to lead people into sin, especially when they are young. But at the same time, seven other spirits were given to humans at creation, which allow them to do good."

1. The first is the spirit of life, which gives strength to the body.

2. The second is the spirit of sight, which brings desire.

3. The third is the spirit of hearing, which allows people to learn.

4. The fourth is the spirit of smell, which enables breathing and the enjoyment of scents.

5. The fifth is the spirit of speech, which allows people to share knowledge.

6. The sixth is the spirit of taste, which makes eating and drinking possible, giving energy.

7. The seventh is the spirit of reproduction, which is meant for love and family but can also lead people into temptation.

"This seventh spirit, though last in creation, is the strongest in youth. It often leads young people into sin without them realizing it, like an animal blindly walking toward a cliff. There is also an eighth spirit, the spirit of sleep, which brings rest but also reminds us of death."

Reuben warned, "These good spirits exist alongside spirits that cause people to sin. The first is the spirit of desire, which takes control of the senses and the body's natural urges. The second is the spirit of greed, which causes people to crave more than they need. The third is the spirit of anger, which is tied to bitterness and jealousy. The fourth is the spirit of deception, which makes false kindness seem real. The fifth is the spirit of arrogance, which leads people to become boastful and proud. The sixth is the spirit of lying, which causes dishonesty, jealousy, and betrayal. The seventh is the spirit of injustice, which leads people to steal and take what does not belong to them. Finally, the spirit of sleep, when mixed with these, confuses young minds and leads them away from truth and God's commandments— just as it happened to me."

"That is why, my children, you must love the truth. It will protect you and keep you safe. Listen to your father, Reuben. Stay away from temptation, do not interfere with another man's wife, and avoid getting caught up in dangerous situations with women."

Reuben then shared his personal experience: "If I had not seen Bilhah bathing in a secluded place, I would never have fallen into such a terrible sin. My mind was overwhelmed by what I saw, and I could not sleep until I acted on my thoughts. When our father Jacob left to visit Isaac in Ephrath near Bethlehem, Bilhah drank too much wine and fell asleep uncovered in her room. I went in, saw her, and committed a great sin without her knowing."

"An angel of God revealed my sin to my father Jacob. He was heartbroken because of me and made a vow never to be with Bilhah again. That is why I warn you, my children—do not let yourselves fall into temptation, because it only leads to regret and destruction."

Chapter II.

Reuben continued sharing his experiences and advice with his children.

"My sons, do not let yourselves be distracted by the beauty of women or become too focused on them. Instead, live with pure hearts, honoring and respecting the Lord. Use your energy to do good, learn, and take care of your work until the Lord chooses a wife for you. That way, you will not face the struggles I did."

"Until my father passed away, I was too ashamed to look him in the eye or speak freely with my brothers. Even now, my conscience still troubles me because of my mistake. But my father was compassionate and prayed for me, asking the Lord to forgive me. The Lord showed me mercy, and His anger was taken away."

"From that time forward, I have been careful and have not sinned again. That is why I urge you, my children, to follow what I have taught you, so you do not fall into the same trap."

"Fornication is a trap for the soul. It pulls people away from God and leads them toward sin. It clouds the mind and weakens good judgment, dragging young men into ruin. It has destroyed many throughout history. No matter if a man is old or young, rich or poor, fornication brings shame and makes him an object of scorn."

"Look at the example of Joseph. He resisted temptation, avoided sinful thoughts, and kept his heart pure. Because of this, he found favor with both God and man. An Egyptian woman tried everything to make him sin. She used magic, false promises, and even trickery, but Joseph stayed strong and did not give in. Because of his faithfulness, God protected him and saved him from hidden danger."

"If you do not allow desire to take over your heart, no evil power can control you. Women, my children, often fall into this sin and use deception to mislead men. Since they do not have the physical strength to overpower men, they rely on their beauty and charm to get what they want. If that does not work, they use more subtle tricks."

"An angel of the Lord revealed to me that women are often more tempted by the spirit of fornication than men. In their hearts, they plan ways to capture a man's attention, using their looks and dress to deceive. First, they take hold of a man's thoughts with their beauty. Then, with a simple glance, they plant temptation in his heart. Once his will is weakened, they trap him in sinful actions. Women cannot force men openly, but they lure them in with their behavior."

"So, my children, avoid fornication at all costs. Teach your wives and daughters not to dress or act in ways that deceive or tempt others. Women who rely on these tricks will face judgment. This same sin led the Watchers astray before the flood. When these heavenly beings saw women and desired them, they changed their forms and pursued them, even though the women were married. The women gave in to temptation and had children with them—giants of great size and strength, almost reaching the heavens."

"Protect yourselves from this sin. If you want to keep your hearts pure, be careful with what you allow yourself to see and hear. Teach women to be modest in how they act around men so they, too, can stay pure in mind and heart. Even if there is no outright sin, too much closeness and familiarity can lead to destruction."

"Fornication does not bring wisdom or godliness. It only causes confusion, jealousy, and rivalry. Because of this, you will become jealous of the sons of Levi and try to elevate yourselves above them, but you will fail. God will defend them, and those who oppose them will face a bitter end."

"God has given leadership to Levi, along with Judah, myself, Dan, and Joseph. But Levi has been given the knowledge of God's law, the authority to judge Israel, and the responsibility to offer sacrifices until the end of time. He will serve as the Lord's High Priest."

"I urge you, by the God of heaven, to be honest with each other and to love your brothers. Respect Levi and approach him with humility so that you may receive his blessing. Levi will bless both Israel and Judah because the Lord has chosen him to be a spiritual leader and king over the nation. Honor his descendants, for they will fight battles for you—both physical and spiritual. And from his family line, an eternal King will come and live among you."

With these words, Reuben finished his teachings. Shortly after, he passed away. His sons placed his body in a coffin and carried it from Egypt to Hebron, where they buried him in the cave beside his father.

Testament of Simeon

The Second Son of Jacob and Leah.

Chapter I.

Simeon, the second son of Jacob and Leah, was known for his great strength. However, he struggled with jealousy and played a major role in the plan against Joseph.

This is what Simeon told his sons as he neared the end of his life at 120 years old, the same year his brother Joseph passed away. When Simeon became seriously ill, his sons gathered around him. Gathering his strength, he sat up, embraced them, and began to speak:

"Listen carefully, my children, to the words of your father, Simeon. I want to share the thoughts that weigh on my heart. I am Jacob's second son, and when I was born, my mother Leah named me Simeon because the Lord heard her prayer. From a young age, I was given great strength. I feared nothing and was never afraid of a challenge. But my heart was hard, my spirit was stubborn, and I lacked compassion."

"God gives people strength, both in body and in spirit, as He chooses. In my youth, jealousy overshadowed my strength. I was filled with envy toward Joseph because our father loved him more than the rest of us. I let this jealousy grow inside me, and I set my heart against Joseph, determined to destroy him. The prince of lies, working through the spirit of jealousy, blinded me. I stopped seeing Joseph as my brother and never considered how much pain I was causing our father, Jacob."

"But the God of Joseph and our ancestors stepped in. He sent His angel to protect Joseph from my hands. I remember the day I went to Shechem to bring ointment for the flocks, and Reuben traveled to Dothan to gather supplies. During that time, Judah sold Joseph to the Ishmaelites. When Reuben found out what happened, he was devastated because he had planned to bring Joseph back to our father."

"When I learned that Judah had let Joseph be taken away alive, I was furious. For five months, I was filled with anger toward Judah for what he had done. But in His mercy, the Lord stopped me from acting on my rage. To humble me, God made my right hand wither for seven days. This suffering helped me realize that I was being punished for what I had done to Joseph."

"I repented with all my heart. I cried, begged for forgiveness, and promised to turn away from envy, impurity, and foolishness. I finally understood that my sin was not just against Joseph but also against the Lord and my father, Jacob."

"So, my children, I beg you to listen carefully to what I am saying. Protect yourselves from envy and deception. Envy can take over a person's heart completely, leaving no room for peace or happiness. It can steal your appetite, make you restless, and drive you to destroy the person you envy. As long as that person succeeds, the envious one remains miserable."

"For two years, I fasted and humbled myself before the Lord in repentance. Only through the fear of God was I freed from envy. When a person trusts in the Lord, the evil spirit of jealousy leaves them, and their heart becomes lighter."

"Once I was freed from envy, I began to feel love and compassion toward Joseph. I forgave him, and I was finally at peace. That is why I urge you to stay away from envy, my children. Only by trusting in God and keeping your hearts free from jealousy can you truly be happy."

Chapter II.

Reuben, the oldest son of Jacob, gave advice to his children and those who would listen, warning them to guard their hearts against jealousy and envy.

"My father once asked me why I always seemed troubled. He saw the sadness in me and wanted to know what was wrong. I told him, 'I am hurting in my liver.' But the truth was, my sorrow ran much deeper than any physical pain. I was carrying the guilt of helping sell my brother Joseph.

When we went to Egypt and Joseph, disguised as an Egyptian ruler, accused me of being a spy and had me tied up, I didn't argue or resist. I knew in my heart that I deserved this. It was a punishment for what I had done.

But Joseph was a man of great kindness, filled with the Spirit of God. He held no grudge against me or any of our brothers. Even after everything we did to him, he still loved us. He treated me like his own family and never sought revenge.

My children, learn from this and protect yourselves from jealousy and envy. Be honest and have a pure heart. Those who live with integrity receive God's grace, honor, and blessings—just like Joseph did. You saw how, despite everything that happened, he never spoke harshly to us. Instead, he loved us deeply, even more than his own children. He gave us wealth, land, and livestock, showing kindness beyond what anyone could expect.

That is why I tell you to love each other sincerely. Let love fill your hearts, and envy will not be able to take hold of you. Envy is like a disease—it eats away at the soul, weakens the body, and stirs up anger. It leads to hatred, violence, and even death. It clouds the mind, fills a person with rage, and causes them to lose control.

Even when a jealous person sleeps, they are not at peace. Like an evil spirit, envy torments the soul, confuses the mind, and disturbs the body. It never stops, always pushing a person toward misery. Wherever envy exists, peace disappears.

Look at Joseph as an example. He was strong, noble, and full of grace because there was no wickedness in him. A person's face often reflects what is inside them, and Joseph's goodness could be seen in his appearance.

Now, my children, keep your hearts pure before the Lord and live honestly with others. If you do this, you will be blessed by God and respected by people. Be especially careful to avoid fornication, for it leads to all kinds of evil. It separates people from God and pulls them toward sin.

I have read in the writings of Enoch that in the future, some of your descendants will fall into fornication and violence, bringing harm to the descendants of Levi. But know this: they will not defeat Levi, for he will rise with the strength of the Lord and fight for what is right. He will overcome all opposition and win the battles that come against him.

In the future, the tribes of Israel will be divided, and only Levi and Judah will remain together. Among your descendants, no one will hold lasting power, just as our father Jacob prophesied. So, my children, take these words to heart. Learn from my mistakes, walk in the ways of righteousness, and do not fall into the traps of envy and sin."

Chapter III.

A prophecy of the coming of the Messiah.

"I have shared all these things with you, my children, so that I am not responsible for any wrongdoing you may commit. If you let go of jealousy and stubbornness, my name will be remembered in Israel like a blooming rose, and my life will be honored in Jacob like a fragrant lily. My memory will be as sweet as the scent of Lebanon, and from my family, strong and holy leaders will rise like mighty cedar trees. Their influence will spread far, and they will endure for generations.

During that time, the descendants of Canaan will disappear, and there will be no survivors among the people of Amalek. The people of Cappadocia will be wiped out, and the Hittites will be completely destroyed. The land of Ham will fall, and its people will vanish.

Then, the earth will finally know peace. The troubles that plague it will come to an end, and wars will cease. The Mighty One of Israel will honor the descendants of Shem, and the Lord God will come to earth to save humankind.

On that day, all lying and deceitful spirits will be crushed and cast away. Wickedness will no longer have power over people, and their suffering will end. When that time comes, I will rejoice and praise the Most High for His great works. I will glorify Him because He will have taken on human form, walked among people, eaten with them, and saved them through His power.

Now, my children, listen carefully. Show respect to the tribes of Levi and Judah, and follow their leadership. Do not rise against them, for from these two will come God's salvation. From Levi, the Lord will bring forth a High Priest, and from Judah, a King—both fully God and fully human. Through them, He will rescue all nations and the people of Israel.

I am giving you these instructions so that you will pass them down to your children and ensure they are followed for generations. Teach them to walk in the ways of the Lord and to honor His plan for salvation.

After Simeon finished speaking, he passed away at the age of 120 years. His sons placed his body in a wooden coffin, planning to carry his remains to Hebron. However, during a war with the Egyptians, they secretly moved his bones because the Egyptians kept a tight guard over Joseph's remains, storing them in the royal tombs.

Egypt's sorcerers had predicted that if Joseph's bones were taken away, a terrible plague would strike their land. Darkness and despair would spread across Egypt, and even with a lamp, people would not be able to recognize their own brothers.

Simeon's sons mourned their father deeply. They remained in Egypt until the time of their great departure, when the Lord kept His promise and, through Moses, led His people to freedom."

Testament of Levi

The Third Son of Jacob and Leah.

Chapter I.

Levi, the third son of Jacob and Leah, was known for his deep spiritual nature, dreams, and prophetic visions. This is the message he gave to his sons, instructing them on how to live and revealing what would happen to them in the future.

Levi was still strong and healthy when he gathered his children because he had been told that his time on earth was coming to an end. When they were all together, he said:

"I, Levi, was born in Haran and later traveled with my father Jacob to Shechem. When I was around twenty years old, I joined my brother Simeon in seeking justice against Hamor and the men of Shechem for dishonoring our sister, Dinah.

Later, while taking care of the flocks in Abel-Maul, the Lord gave me wisdom and understanding. I realized how deeply people had fallen into sin, turning away from what is right. I saw that arrogance had built high walls, and lawlessness ruled from great towers. My heart was troubled, and I prayed to the Lord for help.

As I prayed, I fell into a deep sleep and saw myself standing on a high mountain. Suddenly, the heavens opened, and an angel of God appeared, calling out to me, 'Levi, come forward!'

I followed the angel and was taken up to the first heaven, where I saw a vast sea floating in the air. Amazed, I was then led higher to the second heaven. This place was much brighter, filled with an overwhelming light that stretched endlessly in every direction.

I turned to the angel and asked, 'Why is this heaven so much brighter than the first?' The angel replied, 'Do not be surprised, for you will go even higher and see a place far greater than this. There, you will stand near the Lord. You will serve Him, reveal His mysteries to people, and announce the coming of the One who will save Israel.'

Then the angel said, 'Through you and Judah, the Lord will make Himself known among people, bringing salvation to all nations. The Lord Himself will provide for you—He will be your inheritance, your land, your vineyard, and your wealth.'

The angel then explained what I had seen in the heavens. 'The first heaven looks dark to you because it records all the sins of people. It contains fire, snow, and ice, prepared for the day of God's judgment. There, the spirits of punishment wait for the time when they will carry out God's justice.

The second heaven is where the armies of heaven stand, ready for the day of judgment. They will bring justice against the forces of evil and deception. Above them are the holy ones, set apart by God.

The highest heaven of all is the dwelling place of God's great glory, far above all others in holiness. Just below it is the place where the archangels live. These powerful beings serve before the Lord, praying for the righteous and offering atonement for sins committed in ignorance. Their sacrifices to God are pure and pleasing, requiring no blood.

Below the heaven of the archangels, another group of angels carries messages to those who stand in God's presence. Further down are the thrones and dominions—beings who never stop praising and glorifying God.

When the Lord looks upon creation, everything shakes. The heavens, the earth, and even the deep places tremble before His majesty. Yet people, unaware of these things, continue to sin and offend God without realizing the seriousness of their actions.'"

With these words, Levi finished describing his vision. He urged his sons to live with an awareness of God's power and to take responsibility for the knowledge He had given them.

Chapter II.

Levi spoke with deep passion, urging his sons to stay faithful and seek wisdom, preparing for the day when the Lord will bring judgment.

"My children, understand this—one day, the Lord will judge all people. On that day, the earth will tremble, rocks will split, the sun will grow dark, water will dry up, and even fire will shrink away in fear. Everything in creation will be shaken, and even the hidden spirits will disappear. The underworld will claim those it has taken, and the Most High will bring His power upon the world. Yet, even when these terrifying signs appear, some people will still refuse to believe. They will harden their hearts and continue in their wickedness.

Because of their stubbornness and sins, they will receive the punishment they deserve. But the Most High, in His mercy, has heard your prayers and chosen you to live apart from wickedness. He has called you to be His servant, standing in His presence to do His work.

You are to share wisdom with Jacob's people and shine like the sun for all of Israel's descendants. A great blessing will rest on you and your family, lasting until the day the Lord shows His mercy to all nations and extends His promise forever.

That is why the Lord has given you wisdom and understanding—so that you may teach these truths to your children. Those who honor the Lord will be blessed, but those who reject Him will bring destruction upon themselves.

In a vision, an angel appeared and opened the gates of heaven for me. I saw the holy temple, and on a glorious throne sat the Most High, shining in splendor. He spoke to me, saying, 'Levi, I have given you the blessing of the priesthood. Your descendants will serve Me until the time when I come to live among My people.'

Then, the angel led me back to earth and placed a shield and a sword in my hands. He told me, 'You must bring justice to Shechem for what was done to your sister Dinah. Do not be afraid, for I will be with you. The Lord Himself has sent me to you.'

Following the Lord's command, I led the battle against the sons of Hamor, just as it was written in the heavenly records. Afterward, I asked the angel, 'Tell me your name so I may call on you when I need help.'

The angel answered, 'I am the one who prays for the people of Israel, making sure they are not completely destroyed. Evil spirits are always trying to harm them, but I protect them.'

When I woke up from this vision, I gave thanks and praise to the Most High for His amazing works. I also blessed the angel who prays for Israel and all who follow the Lord, amazed at God's mercy and His care for His people."

Through this powerful story, Levi reminded his children of the importance of their calling and the need to live with faith, righteousness, and obedience to the Lord.

Chapter III.

Levi shared his visions, revealing the incredible rewards that await those who live righteously. His words came from both personal experience and divine revelations.

"When I was returning to my father, I found a bronze shield on a mountain, which I named Aspis. This place is near Gebal, south of Abila. I kept this moment in my heart, thinking about it deeply. Not long after, I advised my father and my brother Reuben to command the sons of Hamor not to be circumcised. My anger burned against them because of what they had done to my sister Dinah.

In my fury, I struck down Shechem first, and Simeon killed Hamor. After that, our brothers joined us, and together we destroyed the city with our swords. When my father Jacob found out, he was deeply troubled. He was upset that the men of Shechem had been circumcised only to be killed afterward. He looked at Simeon and me with disappointment, and we realized that we had disobeyed his will. That day, he became ill with sorrow.

However, I understood that God's judgment had come upon Shechem for their evil ways. They had planned to treat Sarah and Rebecca with the same dishonor they inflicted on Dinah, but the Lord stopped them. Their sins did not start with us—they had troubled Abraham when he stayed in their land, harassing his flocks and mistreating his household. They did the same to all travelers, stealing their wives and dishonoring them. Because of their wickedness, God's punishment fell on them.

I told my father, 'Through you, the Lord will remove the Canaanites from this land and give it to your descendants.' From then on, Shechem became known as the city of fools because they had brought destruction upon themselves.

After we left Shechem, we traveled to Bethel. Seventy days later, I had another vision, similar to the first one I had seen. In my dream, seven men dressed in white robes came to me. They said, 'Levi, rise and put on the robe of the priesthood, the crown of righteousness, the breastplate of understanding, the garment of truth, the plate of faith, the turban for your head, and the ephod of prophecy.'

Each man carried a sacred item, and they placed them on me one by one. Then they declared, 'From now on, you and your descendants will serve as priests to the Lord forever.'

The first man anointed me with holy oil and gave me the staff of judgment. The second man washed me with pure water, gave me bread and wine, and dressed me in a glorious robe. The third man clothed me in a linen vest similar to an ephod. The fourth wrapped a purple sash around my waist. The fifth gave me a branch from a rich olive tree. The sixth placed a crown on my head. Finally, the seventh man placed a priestly diadem on me and filled my hands with incense to offer before the Lord.

Then they spoke, saying, 'Levi, your descendants will be divided into three groups, each carrying a part of the Lord's glory. The first group will be the greatest of all. The second will hold the sacred priesthood. The third will take on a new name because a king will come from Judah and establish a new priesthood, following the ways of the nations. He will be greatly honored because He will be a prophet of the Most High, from the family of Abraham, our ancestor.'

They finished by saying, 'Everything good in Israel will be given to you and your descendants. You will enjoy the Lord's blessings, and your family will serve His people at His holy table.'"

Levi shared his visions and teachings with his children, giving them guidance for their lives and revealing the sacred role their family would play in God's plan.

"Among your descendants, some will become high priests, judges, and scribes. They will be responsible for protecting and keeping the holy place sacred. When I woke up from my dream, I realized it was similar to my first vision. I kept this knowledge in my heart and told no one.

Two days later, Judah and I traveled with our father Jacob to visit our grandfather Isaac. While we were there, Isaac blessed me according to the visions I had seen. He spoke prophetic words over me but chose not to continue the journey with us to Bethel.

When we arrived in Bethel, my father Jacob had a vision about me. In it, he saw that I was meant to serve as a priest for our people. The next morning, he got up early and gave his tithes to the Lord through me, marking the beginning of my sacred calling. From there, we traveled to Hebron and settled there.

Isaac often called me to his side and reminded me of the law of the Lord, as it had been revealed to him and our ancestors. He taught me about the priestly laws and the different kinds of sacrifices—burnt offerings, firstfruits, freewill offerings, and peace offerings. Every day, he instructed me on these sacred duties and prayed for me before the Lord.

Isaac also warned me, saying, 'Be careful of the temptation of impurity, for it will continue through your descendants and bring sin into the holy place.' He advised me to marry a woman of good character, someone pure and without corruption, and not to marry anyone from the foreign nations. He stressed the importance of remaining clean, telling me to wash before entering the holy place, to cleanse myself before making sacrifices, and to wash again after completing the sacrifices.

He also instructed me, 'Take branches from twelve trees that have leaves and offer them to the Lord, as Abraham taught me. From every clean animal and bird, bring sacrifices to God. Offer the firstfruits of your harvest and wine as offerings. And remember, every sacrifice must be seasoned with salt.'

I told my children to follow these commands, saying, 'Everything I have learned from my ancestors, I now pass on to you. I will not be responsible for the sins you commit in the future, especially those against the Savior of the world, Christ. You will act without respect, deceive Israel, and bring great troubles upon it from the Lord. Because of your disobedience, the Lord will no longer protect Jerusalem. The veil in the temple will be torn apart, and your shame will be exposed to the world.'

I warned them further, 'You will be taken as captives among the nations, suffering disgrace because of your actions. However, the city the Lord has chosen will still be called Jerusalem, as it is written in the book of Enoch, the righteous one.'

I shared details of my own life, saying, 'When I was twenty-eight years old, I married a woman named Melcha. She gave birth to my first son, whom I named Gersam, because we were strangers in a foreign land. I had a vision that Gersam would not rise to the highest position among my descendants.

When I was thirty-five, my second son, Kohath, was born at sunrise. In a vision, I saw him standing in an important role among our people, so I named him Kohath, meaning "the beginning of greatness and wisdom."

At forty, my wife gave birth to my third son, Merari, but his birth was very difficult, and she almost died. Because of this, I named him Merari, which means "my sorrow." When I was sixty-four years old, in Egypt, my youngest daughter, Jochebed, was born at a time when I was highly respected among my brothers.

Gersam had two sons, Lomni and Semei. Kohath's sons were Amram, Issachar, Hebron, and Ozeel. Merari's sons were Mooli and Mouses. When I was ninety-four, my grandson Amram married my daughter Jochebed; they were born on the same day.'

I reflected on my life's journey, saying, 'I was eight years old when I entered the land of Canaan, eighteen when I fought against Shechem, and nineteen when I became a priest. At twenty-eight, I got married, and at forty-eight, I moved to Egypt. Now, my children, you are the third generation after me, and in my one hundred and eighteenth year, your uncle Joseph passed away.'

Levi's words were filled with history, visions, and important lessons. He gave his descendants a guide for their future, urging them to stay faithful to God's covenant and to live righteously.

Chapter IV.

Levi spoke with deep wisdom and concern, urging his children to live righteously and wisely while warning them about the consequences of turning away from God. His words were meant to guide them toward a life that honors the Lord and avoids the dangers of sin and rebellion.

"My children, I urge you to fear the Lord with all your heart and follow His law completely. Let your respect for God guide every decision you make, and treasure His commandments above all else.

Teach your children to read and write, so they can understand and carry God's law with them throughout their lives. A person who knows and follows God's law will be respected wherever they go. They will never feel like a stranger, for wisdom brings honor and recognition.

A wise and righteous person will gain more friends than even their parents could provide. Many will seek to serve them, listen to their words, and learn about God's teachings from them. Living righteously is like storing up treasure in heaven, where it is safe forever. If you fill your hearts with goodness, you will enjoy its rewards. But if you fill them with evil, you will only bring trouble upon yourselves.

Seek wisdom with all your heart and trust in God. Unlike wealth, land, or power, wisdom cannot be stolen by enemies or lost in exile. The only things that can destroy wisdom are the blindness that comes from wickedness and the hardness of heart caused by sin. If you protect yourself from these, wisdom will always be your strength, even in difficult times. In a foreign land, wisdom will feel like home, and even among enemies, it will be your ally.

Those who teach truth and live by it will be honored like kings, just as my brother Joseph was. Because of his wisdom and righteousness, Joseph was given great authority and respect.

But my children, I see that in the future, you will turn away from the Lord. You will choose wickedness, and because of your sins, people will mock and despise you. Even though our father Israel remains faithful and pure, the leaders of our people will dishonor our family by mistreating the Savior of the world.

Just as the heavens are purer than the earth in God's eyes, you are meant to be a light to Israel, shining brighter than the nations around you. But if you allow sin to darken your hearts, what hope will there be for those who are already lost in spiritual blindness? By rejecting God's law and creating your own rules, you will bring a curse upon our people.

You will steal what belongs to the Lord, taking offerings meant for Him and wasting them on sinful pleasures. Out of greed, you will twist God's commandments to suit your desires. You will dishonor married women, take advantage of young women, and form sinful relationships. You will marry foreign women and perform false rituals to justify your actions, repeating the sins of Sodom and Gomorrah.

Because of your pride in your priesthood, you will think you are above others, even above God's commands. You will mock what is holy, treating sacred things with laughter and disrespect. Because of this, the Lord will destroy the temple He has chosen, and you will be taken as captives to foreign lands.

Other nations will despise you and mock you. You will bear the shame of God's punishment, and those who hate you will celebrate your downfall. If it weren't for the mercy promised to Abraham, Isaac, and Jacob, not a single one of our descendants would remain on the earth.

For seventy weeks, you will turn away from righteousness, corrupting the priesthood and defiling the sacrifices. You will ignore God's law and reject His prophets. You will mistreat the righteous and hate those who follow God, despising the words of truth.

Then, when a man comes to restore God's law with the power of the Most High, you will call him a liar. You will refuse to recognize who He truly is and will plot to kill Him, staining your hands with innocent blood. Because of this, your holy places will be destroyed, left in ruins.

You will have no place of safety, and you will be scattered among the nations, living under a curse. But one day, the Lord will show mercy again. He will welcome those who turn back to Him in faith, washing them clean and restoring them to His covenant."

Levi's words were both a warning and a promise. He urged his descendants to choose wisdom and righteousness, but he also spoke of God's mercy, which would one day bring them back to Him.

Chapter V.

As you have heard about the seventy weeks, now listen to what will happen with the priesthood. In every generation, there will be priests. In the first generation, the first priest will be great and will speak to God as a son speaks to his father. His priesthood will be perfect before the Lord, and on the day of his greatest joy, he will rise up to bring salvation to the world.

In the second generation, the chosen priest will come from a time of sorrow among loved ones, and his priesthood will be honored and praised by many. The third priest will suffer greatly. The fourth will also endure pain, as wickedness will rise against him, and all of Israel will be filled with hatred, with people turning against each other.

The fifth priest will live in a time of darkness, and the same will happen in the sixth and seventh generations. By the seventh generation, corruption will be so terrible that words cannot even describe it, but those who commit such evil will understand the full weight of their actions. Because of their sins, they will be taken captive, and their land and possessions will be destroyed.

In the fifth week, they will return to their ruined land and rebuild the house of the Lord. By the seventh week, priests will appear who are corrupt, greedy, and immoral. They will worship idols, commit adultery, steal money, act arrogantly, break the law, and defile even children and animals. Because of their evil, the Lord will punish them, and the priesthood will come to an end.

Then, the Lord will raise up a new priest. To this priest, all of God's words will be revealed. He will bring justice to the earth for many days. His star will shine in the heavens like a king's star. He will spread knowledge of the Lord like sunlight covering the earth, and he will be praised throughout the world.

He will shine like the sun, removing all darkness from under the sky. Peace will cover the earth. The heavens will rejoice in his days, and the earth will be glad. Even the clouds will celebrate. The knowledge of the Lord will spread across the earth as abundantly as the waters of the sea.

The angels in heaven will rejoice because of him. The heavens will open, and holiness will come upon him from the temple of glory. The voice of the Father will declare his name, just as it was spoken to Abraham and Isaac. The Most High will reveal his glory over him, and the spirit of wisdom and holiness will rest upon him through water.

He will share the greatness of the Lord with His people forever. No one will take his place for all generations. Through his priesthood, knowledge will spread among the nations, and they will come to know the grace of the Lord. Under his priesthood, sin will come to an end, and lawlessness will be destroyed.

He will open the gates of paradise, removing the sword that blocked the way since the time of Adam. He will allow the righteous to eat from the tree of life, and the spirit of holiness will rest upon them. He will defeat the power of Beliar and give his followers the strength to overcome evil.

The Lord will take joy in His people and be pleased with His chosen ones forever. Abraham, Isaac, and Jacob will rejoice, and I too will be glad, as all the saints are filled with joy.

Now, my children, you have heard everything. It is your choice whether to walk in the light or stay in darkness, whether to follow the law of the Lord or the ways of Beliar.

His sons responded, "We will walk before the Lord and follow His law." Their father said, "The Lord is our witness, His angels are witnesses, and you are witnesses, as I am, to the promise you have made today."

His sons answered, "We are witnesses."

Then Levi finished speaking to his sons. He lay down on his bed, stretched out his feet, and passed away at the age of one hundred and thirty-seven. They placed him in a coffin and later buried him in Hebron with Abraham, Isaac, and Jacob.

The Testament of Judah

The Fourth Son of Jacob and Leah.

Chapter I.

Judah, the fourth son of Jacob and Leah, spoke to his sons before he passed away, sharing his experiences and the lessons he had learned.

"My children, listen to the words of your father, Judah. I was the fourth son born to my father Jacob, and my mother Leah named me Judah, saying, 'I give thanks to the Lord for blessing me with another son.'

In my youth, I was strong, fast, and always obedient to my father. I showed great respect to my mother and her sister. When I became a man, my father blessed me, saying, 'You will be a king and will succeed in everything you do.' The Lord favored me in all my work, both in the fields and at home.

Once, I chased a deer, caught it, and prepared it as a meal for my father, who was pleased. I became skilled in hunting and could outrun and capture any animal in the plains. I even caught and tamed a wild horse.

I once killed a lion and saved a young goat from its jaws. I grabbed a bear by its paw, threw it over a cliff, and crushed it. I outran a wild boar and tore it apart while running. A leopard once attacked my dog in Hebron, but I grabbed it by the tail, slammed it against the rocks, and killed it.

I also came across a wild ox feeding in the fields. I grabbed it by the horns, swung it around, and struck it down. When two kings of the Canaanites came armed to attack our flocks, I faced them alone. I struck the king of Hazor on his armor, pulled him down, and killed him. The king of Tappuah, who was on horseback, I also struck down, scattering his army.

I fought Achor, a giant warrior who threw spears from horseback. I lifted a heavy stone, threw it at his horse, and killed it. I battled him for two hours, broke his shield, cut off his feet, and defeated him. As I was removing his armor, nine of his men attacked me. Wrapping my garment around my arm, I fought back with stones and killed four of them. The rest fled.

My father Jacob once killed Beelesath, the king of all the kings, who was twelve cubits tall and incredibly strong. Fear spread among our enemies, and they stopped waging war against us. My father had no fear in battle when I was with him because he had seen a vision of a powerful angel protecting me, ensuring I would never be defeated.

A greater war than the one at Shechem came upon us in the south. I joined my brothers in battle, chasing a thousand men and killing two hundred, including four kings. I climbed the city wall and killed four strong warriors. We captured Hazor and took its treasures.

The next day, we marched to Aretan, a heavily fortified city that was a threat to us. Gad and I attacked from the east, while Reuben and Levi came from the west. The men on the wall, thinking we were alone, came down to fight us. Meanwhile, my brothers secretly climbed the wall, entered the city, and struck down the warriors.

We burned their tower and took control of the city. As we were leaving, the men of Tappuah attacked, trying to steal our spoils. We fought them, defeated them, and reclaimed everything. At the waters of Kozeba, the men of Jobel waged war against us. We defeated them and their allies from Shiloh, making them too weak to attack us again.

On the fifth day, the men of Makir came to take our spoils. We met them in battle, overcame their strongest warriors, and killed them before they could retreat up the hill. When we reached their city, the women rolled stones down from the hilltop to stop us. Simeon and I circled behind the town, took the high ground, and destroyed the city.

The next day, we learned that the king of Gaash was advancing with a powerful army. Dan and I disguised ourselves as Amorites and entered their city as allies. In the middle of the night, our brothers arrived, and we opened the gates for them. We defeated the men, destroyed their defenses, and took their possessions.

We then moved to Thamna, where the treasures of many enemy kings were stored. When they insulted us, I became angry and charged up the hill, even as they threw stones and arrows at me. Dan came to help, and together we drove them away. They fled and later fought my father Jacob, but he made peace with them. We did not harm them further, and they became subject to us. We returned their possessions and restored order.

I built Thamna, and my father built Pabael. I was twenty years old during these wars, and the Canaanites feared me and my brothers. I had many herds and put Iram the Adullamite in charge of them. While visiting him, I met Parsaba, the king of Adullam. He welcomed us and hosted a great feast.

During the feast, he gave me his daughter Bathshua as my wife. She bore me three sons: Er, Onan, and Shelah. However, the Lord took the lives of Er and Onan, leaving only Shelah, whose descendants remain with you now."

Chapter II.

For eighteen years, my father Jacob lived in peace with his brother Esau and Esau's sons after we returned from Mesopotamia, where we had stayed with Laban. But when those eighteen years passed, in the fortieth year of my life, Esau and his men attacked us with a strong and well-armed army.

During the battle, my father Jacob shot an arrow at Esau, wounding him. Esau was taken back to Mount Seir, where he later died at a place called Anoniram. We chased after Esau's sons, who had built a city with iron walls and brass gates. Since we couldn't break through, we set up camp around the city and laid siege to it.

For twenty days, they refused to open the gates. Then, in full view of everyone, I climbed a ladder with my shield protecting me, while they threw large stones down at me. Even though the stones were heavy, I managed to kill four of their strongest warriors. Reuben and Gad killed six more. After this, the people inside the city surrendered and asked for peace. After speaking with our father, we agreed to make them our subjects. They were required to send us five hundred cors of wheat, five hundred baths of oil, and five hundred measures of wine every year. This continued until the famine forced us to go down to Egypt.

Later, my son Er married Tamar, a woman from Mesopotamia and a daughter of Aram. But Er was a wicked man and treated her badly because she was not from Canaan. Three days after their wedding, an angel of the Lord struck him down. He had never been with her because his mother had convinced him not to let Tamar bear his children.

During the wedding, I gave Tamar to my other son, Onan. But Onan also acted wickedly. He lived with her for a year but refused to be with her properly. When I confronted him, he pretended to listen, but he still disobeyed. He wasted his seed instead of allowing her to conceive, following his mother's instructions. Because of this, the Lord struck him down too.

I planned to give Tamar to my youngest son, Shelah, as his wife, but his mother refused. She schemed against Tamar because she disliked her for not being a Canaanite, just as she herself was. I knew the people of Canaan were wicked, but in my youth, I had been blinded by my desires.

She tricked me into marrying her by getting me drunk on wine, even though my father Jacob had not approved. While I was away, she secretly arranged for Shelah to marry a Canaanite woman. When I found out, I was heartbroken and angry. In my grief, I cursed her. Her wickedness eventually led to her death, as well as the deaths of her sons.

Meanwhile, Tamar remained a widow. After two years, she heard that I was going to shear my sheep, so she dressed herself as a bride and sat at the city gate in Enaim. Among the Amorites, it was a custom for a woman about to marry to sit at the gate for seven days.

I was drunk with wine and did not recognize her. Her beauty deceived me, and I approached her, saying, "Let me be with you." She asked what I would give in return, and I handed her my staff, my belt, and my royal diadem as a pledge. I was with her that night, and she became pregnant.

Later, not knowing what had happened, I wanted to punish her and even considered putting her to death. But she secretly sent back my pledges, proving that I was the one responsible. This shamed me deeply. When I summoned her, she repeated the private words I had spoken to her when I was drunk. I realized this was from the Lord and could not harm her.

I thought she might have acted cleverly, but she had taken the pledge directly from me, not from someone else. From that moment on, I never went near her again, knowing I had committed a terrible mistake.

The people of the city claimed that no prostitute had been at the gate because Tamar was not from the city and had only stayed there briefly. I thought my actions had gone unnoticed.

After this, we went down to Egypt because of the famine. I was forty-six years old when we arrived there, and I lived in Egypt for seventy-three more years.

Chapter III.

Listen carefully, my children, and follow my advice. Obey God's laws and keep His commands. Do not let your desires or pride lead your decisions. Do not brag about your strength or accomplishments, because such arrogance is not pleasing to God.

I used to think I was strong enough to resist temptation. I even scolded my brother Reuben for his sin. But jealousy and desire tested me, and I made mistakes with Bathshua, a Canaanite woman, and Tamar, who was meant to marry my sons.

When I wanted to marry Bathshua, I told her father I would first ask my own father. But he didn't want to wait. Instead, he showed off his wealth and offered it in her name. He was a king, and he covered her in gold and jewels. Then, at a feast, he gave us wine and used her beauty to tempt me.

The wine clouded my judgment, and my desires took over. I fell in love with her, slept with her, and broke God's commands. I married her, but God punished me for my mistakes. I found no happiness in the children she gave me.

So, my children, I warn you: do not drink too much wine. It confuses the mind and stirs up dangerous desires. It makes you see things the wrong way and weakens your self-control. Wine can trick you into thinking you are happy while it actually leads you to sin.

When a man gets drunk, his mind fills with sinful thoughts, and his body craves wicked things. If the opportunity arises, he will sin without shame. A drunk person loses all respect for others.

I let wine lead me into sin. I publicly shamed myself and my family when I turned to Tamar. I ignored God's laws and married a Canaanite woman, which was against His will.

Be very careful with wine. Drink only in moderation, with respect for God. If you go too far, it will control your mind and fill you with deceit. A drunk man speaks shameful words, sins without regret, and even thinks his disgrace is something to be proud of.

A man who gives in to desire is blind to what he is losing. Even a king who falls into lust will lose his power and become a slave to his own urges. I know this from experience. When I gave Tamar my staff, my belt, and my crown, I lost symbols of my strength and honor.

I repented, but I suffered greatly. From that time on, I avoided wine and meat for the rest of my life, and I found little joy. God's angel showed me that women can have power over all men—kings, warriors, and even the poor. They can take away a king's glory, a strong man's power, and a poor man's last bit of hope.

So, my children, remember the dangers of wine. It carries four great evils: lust, reckless desire, foolishness, and greed. Drink with joy, but always with respect for God. If you forget Him while drinking, you will fall into sin.

If you truly want to live righteously, it is better to avoid wine completely. Drunkenness leads to fights, insults, and rebellion against

God. It can ruin your life too soon. Wine also makes people reveal secrets—both human and divine. I foolishly told God's commandments and my father Jacob's wisdom to Bathshua, though I was not supposed to.

Wine causes confusion and conflict. My children, I warn you: do not let greed or attraction control you. These things led me astray, and I know they will bring trouble to my descendants. Because of them, Judah's kingdom will suffer, even though God blessed me with it for obeying my father.

I never disobeyed my father Jacob. I followed all his commands, and my grandfather Isaac blessed me to be king over Israel. Jacob confirmed this blessing. I know my family's kingdom will continue, but I also know the sins you will commit in the future.

Beware of lust and greed. These sins will turn you away from God, blind your soul, make you arrogant, and destroy your kindness. They fill your life with stress and misery, robbing you of peace. They stop you from worshiping, make you forget God's blessings, and turn you against His teachings.

A man controlled by these desires cannot serve God. He walks in darkness, even in daylight. Greed is like idolatry—it makes people trust money instead of God and drives them to madness.

Because of money, I lost my children. If I had not repented and prayed, I would have died without a family. But God showed me mercy because I sinned in ignorance. I was blinded by deception, and through my mistakes, I learned how weak I truly was.

My children, understand that two spirits guide every person: the spirit of truth and the spirit of deceit. In between is the spirit of understanding, which helps a man choose his path. Everything we do is recorded in our hearts, and God sees it all.

No deed is hidden from Him. The spirit of truth witnesses everything, and a sinner is judged by his own heart, unable to lift his face before God.

The Testament of Issachar

The Fifth Son of Jacob and Leah.

Chapter I.

Issachar, the fifth son of Jacob and Leah, was known for his humble nature and simple way of life.

He gathered his sons and said, "Listen to me, your father Issachar, and pay attention to my words, for I am loved by the Lord. I was born as Jacob's fifth son because my mother made a deal with Rachel in exchange for mandrakes.

One day, my brother Reuben found mandrakes in the field. Rachel saw them and took them, which upset Reuben, and he cried loudly. My mother, Leah, heard his cries and came outside. Mandrakes are fragrant fruits, similar to apples, that grow near water in the land of Haran.

Rachel refused to give them back, saying, 'I need these as a substitute for the children I have not had. God has not given me any sons.'

There were two mandrakes, and Leah argued, 'Isn't it enough that you took my husband? Now you want these too?' Rachel replied, 'I will let you have Jacob with you tonight in exchange for the mandrakes.'

Leah insisted, 'Jacob is my husband. I was with him from the beginning.' But Rachel said, 'Don't be so proud. Jacob worked fourteen years to marry me, and I was meant to be his wife before you. If it weren't for the lies and deceit of others, you would not have been given to him instead of me. My father tricked both of us that night. If I had been there, none of this would have happened.'

Despite this, Rachel said, 'For the sake of the mandrakes, I will give Jacob to you for one night.' That night, Jacob was with Leah, and she became pregnant with me. Since she had used the mandrakes to secure time with Jacob, she named me Issachar.

Later, an angel appeared to Jacob and told him, 'Rachel will have two sons because she has chosen to live in self-control rather than chasing after Jacob with selfish desires.' If Leah had not given up the mandrakes to be with Jacob, she would have had eight sons instead of six. The Lord allowed Rachel to have two children because of the mandrakes.

God saw that Leah wanted to be with Jacob not for her own pleasure but to continue his family line. Because of her selflessness, I was born, and Jacob's family continued to grow."

The next day, Rachel once again allowed Leah to be with Jacob because of the mandrakes. Though she had wanted them, Rachel did not eat them. Instead, she offered them to God and gave them to the priest at the Lord's house.

As I grew up, my children, I lived an honest and simple life. I worked in the fields for my father and brothers, harvesting food at the right times. My father saw my integrity and blessed me.

I never meddled in others' affairs or felt jealous of my neighbors. I did not gossip or judge how others lived. I kept my heart pure and my conscience clear.

When I turned thirty-five, I got married. By then, years of work had worn me down, and I had not spent my time chasing pleasure or thinking about women. I was so focused on my work that I would often fall asleep exhausted.

My father, Jacob, was proud of me because I always gave the first portion of my harvest to God through the priest and then brought the rest to him. The Lord blessed my efforts, and my crops multiplied greatly. My father knew this was because my heart was pure and honest before God.

I shared freely with the poor and those in need, always giving with kindness and sincerity.

Now, my children, listen to me and live with honesty and integrity, for I have seen how much the Lord loves those with pure hearts. Such people do not crave riches or take advantage of others. They are not obsessed with fine food or luxury. They do not fear death but trust in God's plan for their lives.

Those with pure hearts cannot be controlled by deceitful spirits. They avoid looking at things that could lead them into temptation or corrupt their thoughts. They do not hold grudges, feel jealous, or become consumed by worldly desires.

They live truthfully, guided by a clear conscience. They avoid sin and stay faithful to God's commandments.

So, my children, obey God's laws and live with honesty and simplicity. Do not interfere in other people's business. Instead, love God and care for those around you. Show kindness to the poor and weak.

Work hard, especially in farming, and always give thanks to God for your blessings. Offer the first part of your harvest to Him, and He will reward you, just as He has blessed His faithful servants since the time of Abel.

Remember, the land itself is your inheritance. It will provide for you through hard work.

Jacob, our father, blessed me with the abundance of the earth, and God showed His favor by giving me good harvests. Among our family, the Lord gave special roles to Levi and Judah. Levi was chosen to serve as a priest and lead our people spiritually. Judah was given the role of ruler and protector of Israel.

Honor and respect these chosen ones of the Lord. Live with the same sincerity and integrity that I have shown, for it is through a pure heart that God's blessings will remain with you.

Know that Gad has been chosen by God to protect Israel. He will rise up against our enemies and keep our people safe, as the Lord has commanded.

Chapter II.

Your descendants will one day turn away from the simple and pure way of life that pleases the Lord. Instead of being content, they will always want more, chasing after their desires without satisfaction.

They will abandon honesty and sincerity, choosing instead to follow deceit and evil. Ignoring God's commandments, they will be drawn toward wickedness, following the path of the deceiver. Hard work and caring for the land will no longer matter to them. Instead, they will focus only on their own selfish plans.

Because of these sins, they will be scattered among foreign nations and forced to serve their enemies. Their disobedience will take them far from God's blessings, and they will suffer under those who rule over them.

So, my children, teach these warnings to your own children. If they fall into sin, they must return to the Lord quickly. God is merciful and full of compassion. If they cry out to Him, He will hear them, free them from their suffering, and bring them back to their land—if they truly repent.

I am now 126 years old, and I stand before you with a clear conscience. As far as I know, I have not committed any sin. I have been faithful to my wife and have never been with another woman. I never let my eyes lead me into lust or sin.

I avoided drinking wine, so it would not cloud my judgment. I did not desire what belonged to others, and I never allowed deceit to take root in my heart. I have never spoken lies.

Whenever I saw someone struggling, I shared in their pain and sorrow. I gave food to the poor and lived with kindness and faith in God every day. I have always walked in truth, loving the Lord with all my heart and treating others with the same sincerity and care.

My children, I urge you to live as I have. If you follow this way of life, every evil spirit will flee from you, and no wicked person will have power over you. Even wild animals will not harm you, because the God of heaven and earth will be with you. You will live among others with honesty and a pure heart.

After saying these things, I gave my last instructions to my sons. I told them to carry my body to Hebron and bury me in the cave with my ancestors. Then, having spoken my final words, I lay down peacefully and passed away. I lived a long life, still strong in body, and entered the eternal rest that the Lord had prepared for me.

The Testament of Zebulun

The Sixth Son of Jacob and Leah.

Chapter I.

Zebulun, the sixth son of Jacob and Leah, shared his final teachings with his sons two years after Joseph's death, at the age of 114.

He gathered his children and said, "Listen to me, my sons, and hear the words of your father, Zebulun. When I was born, I was a blessing to my parents. After my birth, my father Jacob's wealth increased greatly. His flocks and herds multiplied, especially because of the striped rods he used to claim his share of the livestock.

Throughout my life, I have not knowingly committed any sins, except for those in my thoughts. Even then, I can only recall one major wrongdoing—the time I went along with my brothers in keeping Joseph's fate a secret from our father. In my heart, I grieved for many days, but I was too afraid to speak up. My brothers had made a pact that anyone who revealed the truth would be killed.

When they first plotted to kill Joseph, I begged them with tears not to do such a terrible thing. Simeon and Gad were ready to strike him down, but Joseph pleaded with them, saying, 'Please, my brothers, have mercy on me! Think of our father Jacob and do not spill innocent blood. I have done nothing against you. If I have sinned, then punish me, but do not take my life—it would break our father's heart.'

His cries were unbearable. I wept with him, my heart aching so much that I could barely stand. Joseph saw me crying beside him, and when he realized that our brothers were closing in to kill him, he ran behind me for protection, begging me to save him.

At that moment, Reuben stepped in and said, 'Do not kill him. Instead, throw him into this dry pit.' These pits had been dug by our forefathers but had never filled with water. By God's design, this saved Joseph's life.

My brothers agreed and threw Joseph into the pit. Later, they sold him to the Ishmaelites. I took no part in the money they received for him, but Simeon, Gad, and six of our other brothers used it to buy sandals for themselves and their families. They said, 'We will not eat food purchased with this money, for it was paid with our brother's blood. Instead, we will walk on it, just as Joseph claimed he would rule over us. Let's see what happens to his dreams now.'

Their actions were later reflected in the law of Moses, which says that if a man refuses to raise children for his brother, his sandal should be taken from him, and he should be publicly shamed. In the same way, our brothers rejected Joseph, and God stripped them of the authority they had once held over him.

Years later, when they arrived in Egypt, Joseph's servants removed their sandals at the palace gates, and they bowed before him as they would before Pharaoh. Not only did they bow, but they were also humiliated, spit upon, and forced to the ground in shame. When the Egyptians learned how they had treated Joseph, they condemned them for their cruelty.

After selling Joseph, my brothers sat down to eat and drink, but I could not bring myself to join them. I felt too much pity for Joseph. Instead, I stayed near the pit, afraid that Simeon, Dan, or Gad might try to harm him. Seeing that I would not eat, my brothers put me in charge of watching over him until the Ishmaelites arrived.

When Reuben returned later and found out that Joseph had been sold, he tore his clothes in grief and cried, 'How can I face our father now?' He took the money and ran after the merchants, hoping to buy Joseph back, but he could not find them. They had already taken a shortcut through the land of the Troglodytes. Reuben returned to us heartbroken and refused to eat for the rest of the day.

Dan tried to calm him, saying, 'Do not weep. We have a plan to explain everything to our father. We will kill a young goat and dip Joseph's coat in its blood. Then we will send it to Jacob with the message: Is this your son's coat?'

When Joseph was sold, my brothers took his coat and dressed him as a slave. Simeon kept the coat for himself, refusing to let it go. In anger, he wanted to tear it apart with his sword because Joseph was still alive.

The rest of us turned against Simeon and warned him, 'If you do not hand over the coat, we will tell our father that you alone were responsible for what happened to Joseph.'

Reluctantly, he gave it up, and we carried out Dan's plan. We sent the bloodied coat to Jacob, making him believe that Joseph had been killed by a wild animal."

Chapter II.

Zebulun, the sixth son of Jacob and Leah, urged his children to live with kindness, unity, and mercy, sharing the lessons he had learned throughout his life.

He told them, "My children, I ask you to follow God's commandments. Be kind to your neighbors and show compassion to all living things—not just people, but also animals under your care. Because of this kindness, God has blessed me greatly. When my brothers fell sick, I was the only one who remained healthy, for the Lord sees what is in each person's heart.

Let compassion guide your actions. Whatever kindness you show to others, God will return to you. Many of my brothers' children became ill and died because they lacked mercy for Joseph. But my own children remained healthy, as you yourselves have seen.

When I lived by the sea in Canaan, I became a fisherman to provide for my father Jacob. Many people drowned in the sea, but the Lord kept me safe. I was the first among us to build a boat and sail the waters, for God gave me the wisdom to do so. I designed a rudder to steer the boat and raised a sail on a mast. With these, I traveled along the shores, catching fish to feed our family until we moved to Egypt.

Because of the kindness in my heart, I shared what I caught with anyone in need. If someone was a stranger, sick, or old, I would cook the fish, prepare them well, and offer them to him. I grieved with those who were suffering and tried to ease their burdens. Because of this, God always blessed my fishing. Whoever gives generously to others will receive even more from the Lord in return.

For five years, I fished and gave to the poor, providing enough to sustain not only them but also my father's household. In the summer, I worked as a fisherman, and in the winter, I took care of the sheep alongside my brothers.

There is one act of kindness I want to tell you about. One winter, I saw a man shivering from the cold because he had no clothes. Feeling deep compassion, I secretly took a garment from my father's house and gave it to him. My children, let this be an example for you. From everything God gives you, be quick to show kindness. Give freely to anyone in need with a willing and joyful heart.

Even if you have nothing to give, do not turn away from those who are suffering. Walk with them, share in their pain, and let them know they are not alone. There was a time when I had no way to help a man in distress, so I walked beside him for seven furlongs, crying with him and wishing I could ease his burden.

My children, be compassionate to everyone, and God will be compassionate to you when you are in need. In the last days, He will pour out His mercy upon the earth, and wherever He finds hearts filled with kindness, He will be with them. God's mercy for a person will always match the mercy they have shown to others.

Remember Joseph. Even after all we did to him, he did not seek revenge. Follow his example. Be free of hatred, love one another, and do not hold grudges. Resentment destroys families, troubles the soul, and weakens the spirit.

Think about how a river flows. When its waters are united, they are strong enough to carry stones, trees, and even the earth itself. But when the river breaks into small streams, the water dries up and disappears. The same will happen to you if you let divisions grow among you.

Do not let yourselves be torn apart. Everything in creation has one head and works together as a single body—two shoulders, two hands, two feet, and so on. I have read in the writings of my ancestors that Israel will one day be divided. You will follow two kings and commit terrible sins. Because of this, your enemies will take you captive, and you will suffer among foreign nations, facing disease and hardship.

But even then, you will remember the Lord and repent. He is merciful and forgiving. He does not hold onto anger forever, knowing that people are weak and easily led astray. When you return to Him, the Lord will rise as the light of righteousness. You will return to your land and see Him in Jerusalem, for His name's sake.

Yet even after this, you will fall into sin again and make Him angry. He will cast you away until the time comes for everything to be fulfilled.

Now, my children, do not be sad that my time is near. Do not grieve because I am leaving you. I will rise again among my descendants as a ruler, and I will rejoice with those in my tribe who follow God's commandments. But for those who choose wickedness, the Lord will bring eternal fire, and their families will be destroyed.

My time has come to rest, just as it did for my fathers before me. Honor the Lord with all your strength and remain faithful to Him throughout your lives."

After saying these words, Zebulun passed away peacefully at an old age. His sons placed his body in a wooden coffin and later carried him to Hebron, where they buried him with his ancestors.

The Testament of Dan

The Seventh Son of Jacob and Bilhah.

Chapter I.

Dan, the seventh son of Jacob and Bilhah, spoke these words to his sons near the end of his life when he was 125 years old.

He gathered his family and said, "Listen closely, my sons, to the words of your father. Pay attention to the lessons I share, for they come from my life's experiences and the truths I have learned. I have seen that honesty and fairness bring blessings from the Lord, while lies and anger lead only to destruction and wickedness.

I must confess to you, my children, that I once allowed jealousy and anger to take hold of my heart. I wanted to kill my brother Joseph, even though he was good and truthful. When he was sold into slavery, I felt joy because I envied him. Our father loved him more than the rest of us, and it hurt my pride. A voice inside me whispered, 'Are you not also Jacob's son? Don't you deserve the same love?'

One of the spirits of deception urged me to take a sword and end Joseph's life. It convinced me that if he were gone, our father would love me more. This was the spirit of anger, pushing me to destroy Joseph, just as a wild animal crushes its prey.

But God did not allow me to carry out my evil plan. I was never able to find Joseph alone, and I was stopped from harming him. If I had succeeded, I would have destroyed one of the tribes of Israel.

Now, as my life comes to an end, I warn you: if you do not guard yourselves against lying and anger, you will destroy yourselves. Anger blinds the heart and mind, making it impossible to see the truth in others.

An angry person treats even his own parents as enemies. He no longer recognizes his own brother, ignores the words of wise men, and has no respect for the righteous. Even a close friend becomes like a stranger to him. Anger traps a person in lies, twisting his thoughts and filling his heart with hatred and jealousy.

My children, anger is a dangerous thing. It takes over the soul and controls the body, pushing it toward wrongdoing. As the body follows anger's commands, the soul becomes blind and starts justifying its actions, believing them to be right.

A man with power who is full of anger is even more dangerous. His rage is strengthened in three ways: first, by those who serve him and carry out his orders; second, by his wealth, which he uses to harm others; and third, by his physical strength, which he uses to do evil. Even a weak man becomes more dangerous when fueled by anger, because rage multiplies his ability to do harm.

Anger is closely connected to lies, and together they lead people into cruelty and deception. My children, understand that anger is a useless and destructive force. It starts with harsh words, grows into harmful actions, and fills the mind with rage and confusion.

When someone insults you, do not let anger take hold of you. And when someone praises you, do not let it make you proud. Do not let either praise or insult control your emotions, for both can be traps. At first, compliments feel good, making a person search for reasons to feel important. But later, when insulted, an angry person believes his rage is justified.

If you experience loss or hardship, do not let it trouble your heart. Anger uses disappointment to make people crave things they do not have, leading to frustration and rage. Whether you lose something by choice or by accident, do not let it disturb your peace. Frustration fuels anger, and anger invites lies, forming a destructive cycle.

When anger and lies work together, they fill the heart with constant turmoil. A soul caught in this cycle drives away the presence of the Lord, allowing deception to take control instead.

My children, guard your hearts against the power of anger. Instead, choose patience, truth, and kindness, for these are the ways of the Lord. They bring peace and strength to the soul. Anger blinds, divides, and destroys, but righteousness and love bring unity and lasting strength."

Chapter II.

Listen carefully, my children, and take these words to heart. Follow God's commandments and live according to His law. Stay away from anger and the rejection of truth. If you do this, you will create a place where the Lord can dwell among you, and the deceiver, Beliar, will have no power over you.

Always speak truthfully to one another. Truth protects you from confusion and anger. When you live in honesty, you will remain at peace because the God of peace will be with you, and no enemy will be able to defeat you.

Love the Lord with all your heart and soul, and love each other sincerely. This love will unite you and protect you during difficult times.

But I see that in the future, many of you will turn away from God. Some of you will rebel against Levi and fight against Judah, but you will not succeed. An angel of the Lord will guide Levi and Judah, and through their strength, Israel will stand firm.

When you abandon God, you will fall into sin. You will follow the ways of foreign nations, chasing after wickedness and acting without restraint. Pride and deception will lead you into wrongdoing.

I have read in the writings of Enoch, the righteous man, that Satan will work alongside these spirits of evil to corrupt the sons of Levi, leading them to sin against the Lord. My own descendants will also fall into sin and join Levi in their wrongdoings. Meanwhile, the sons of Judah will become greedy, taking what does not belong to them, like lions devouring their prey.

Because of these sins, you will be taken into captivity. You will suffer plagues like those in Egypt and endure hardships under foreign nations. But even in your suffering, if you turn back to the Lord, He will show you mercy. He will bring you home to His sanctuary and restore peace to you once again.

From the tribes of Judah and Levi, the Lord will send a Savior. He will fight against Beliar and defeat him, bringing justice against our enemies. He will rescue the souls of the faithful from the grasp of evil and turn the hearts of the disobedient back to God. Those who call upon Him will find eternal peace.

The righteous will find rest in Eden, and the faithful will rejoice in the New Jerusalem. This city will forever bring glory to God. No longer will Jerusalem be empty, and no longer will Israel be taken captive. The Lord Himself will live among His people. The Holy One of Israel will reign with humility, and those who believe in Him will rule in truth.

Fear the Lord, my children, and be careful not to fall into Satan's traps. Stay close to God and to the angel who watches over you, for he stands between God and man, working for Israel's peace and fighting against the enemy's kingdom.

The enemy wants to destroy those who call on the Lord because he knows that when Israel repents, his power will be broken. The angel of peace will strengthen Israel, preventing them from completely falling into evil, even in times of great corruption.

Even when Israel turns away from righteousness, the Lord will not abandon them forever. Instead, He will reshape them into a nation that fulfills His purpose. His name will be known not only in Israel but also among the nations.

So, my children, stay away from all evil. Let go of anger and lies, and hold onto truth and patience. Live according to the teachings I have given you and pass them down to your children. Then, when the Savior of the nations comes, He will accept you. He is truthful, patient, humble, and kind, teaching the law of God through His actions.

Turn away from wickedness and follow the righteousness of the Lord. If you do this, your descendants will be saved forever.

Bury me with my fathers, for I wish to rest beside them.

After saying these words, he kissed his sons, lay down, and passed away peacefully at an old age. His sons buried him, and later, they carried his bones to be placed near Abraham, Isaac, and Jacob.

Yet, even in his final moments, Dan warned that his descendants would turn away from God. They would lose their place in the land of their ancestors, become distant from the people of Israel, and be cut off from their family's inheritance.

The Testament of Naphtali

The Eighth Son of Jacob and Bilhah.

Chapter I.

Naphtali, the eighth son of Jacob and Bilhah, shared his final teachings with his sons as his life neared its end. At the age of 130, he gathered his children on the first day of the seventh month to pass down his wisdom.

While still in good health, he prepared a feast of food and wine for his family. The next morning, he woke and said, "My time is near." His sons did not believe him because he still appeared strong. But as he praised and glorified the Lord, his strength increased, and he repeated that he would soon pass away. Then, he began to speak:

"My sons, listen to the words of your father, Naphtali. I was born to Bilhah, and Rachel gave me my name. She had given Bilhah to Jacob in her place, and when I was born on Rachel's knees, she named me Naphtali. She loved me dearly and would often kiss me, saying, 'May I one day have a son of my own who is like you.'

Joseph, my brother, was indeed like me, fulfilling Rachel's prayers. My mother, Bilhah, was the daughter of Rotheus, the brother of Deborah, who was Rebecca's nurse. She was born on the same day as Rachel and came from a noble, God-fearing family that descended from Abraham. Rotheus, however, was captured and sold as a slave to Laban. Laban gave him Euna, a servant, as a wife.

Euna gave birth to Zilpah, naming her after the place where Rotheus was captured. Later, she had Bilhah, saying, 'My daughter is quick to take to new things,' because Bilhah eagerly reached for her mother's breast.

Like my mother, I too was swift. I was as fast as a deer, and my father Jacob trusted me to deliver all his important messages. He blessed me as a fast runner, comparing me to a deer.

The Lord is like a potter, shaping each person with care and intention. Every body is designed to match the spirit it holds, and nothing is created without purpose. Everything in creation is made with precision—perfectly measured and balanced.

Just as a potter knows the use of each vessel he makes, God knows the strengths and weaknesses of every person. He sees how far someone will go in righteousness and when they may turn to evil. Nothing is hidden from Him, for He created everyone in His image.

A person's strength reflects their actions. Their eyes affect their rest, and their soul determines the words they speak—whether they follow God's law or the ways of wickedness. Just as light and darkness are separate, so is every person unique, created exactly as God intended.

God made everything in an orderly way. He placed the senses in the head, covering it with hair as a sign of dignity. The neck connects the head to the body, the heart is for wisdom, the stomach for nourishment, the liver for anger, the gall for bitterness, and the spleen for laughter. Every part of the body has a purpose, designed by God's will.

Therefore, my children, let all your actions be done with order and purpose. Do nothing with bad intentions or at the wrong time. Just as an eye cannot hear, you cannot walk in the ways of light while living in darkness.

Guard yourselves against greed and deceitful words that can lead the soul astray. Keep your hearts pure, and know when to remain silent. If you do, you will understand God's will and reject the ways of evil.

The sun, moon, and stars never leave their assigned paths, and neither should you stray from God's commandments. Do not live in disorder, as the Gentiles have done. They have turned away from the Lord, worshiping idols and following deceitful spirits. Do not be like them. See God's presence in the heavens, the earth, and the seas, and in all creation. Do not follow the ways of Sodom, which went against the natural order.

Even the Watchers, the fallen ones, defied the order God had set for them. Because of their sins, they were cursed and brought destruction to the earth before the flood. I share this warning because I have read in the writings of Enoch that you, too, will one day turn away from God. You will follow the wickedness of the nations and fall into the same sins as Sodom.

Because of this, the Lord will allow your enemies to take you captive. You will suffer, serving foreign nations, until He has humbled you. But when you are reduced in number and remember the Lord, you will return to Him, and in His mercy, He will restore you to the land of your ancestors.

Yet even after returning, you will again forget the Lord and fall into sin. Because of this, He will scatter you across the earth until, in His compassion, He sends a man who will bring righteousness and mercy to both those who are near and those who are far away."

The Testament of Gad

The Ninth Son of Jacob and Zilpah.

Chapter I.

Gad, the ninth son of Jacob and Zilpah, shared his final words with his children as his life neared its end. At the age of 125, he gathered them together to pass down the lessons he had learned, speaking with honesty and a sincere desire to help them avoid the mistakes he had made.

"My sons," he said, "listen to me carefully. I was the ninth son of Jacob, and I was known for my strength and courage as a shepherd. It was my responsibility to guard our flocks, keeping them safe from wild animals. Whenever a lion, wolf, or any predator came near, I would chase it down without fear. I would grab its foot, throw it to the ground, and kill it to protect the flock.

When my brother Joseph came to help tend the sheep, he stayed with us for over a month. But he was young and not used to the heat, so he became sick and returned to Hebron, where our father cared for him with great love. While he was there, Joseph told our father that the sons of Zilpah and Bilhah, including me, were taking the best of the flock and eating them, despite the warnings of Reuben and Judah.

One day, Joseph saw me pull a lamb from the jaws of a bear. Though I killed the bear, I was heartbroken that the lamb did not survive, so we ate it. Joseph reported this to our father, and from that moment, I held resentment toward him. My anger grew stronger over time, and by the day he was sold into slavery, it had completely taken over my heart.

Hatred took root in me, and I no longer wanted to hear Joseph's name or see his face. I hated when he corrected us, and I resented how our father always believed him. The bitterness inside me became so strong that I even wished for his death. My heart was filled with rage, and I wanted him gone, as an ox eats up the grass.

But Judah secretly sold Joseph to the Ishmaelites, and God prevented us from committing an even greater sin. Because of this,

Joseph was saved from our hands, and we were spared from committing a terrible crime.

Now, my children, listen to me and choose truth and righteousness. Stay far away from hatred, for it destroys everything good. A person ruled by hatred cannot see clearly and despises even those who do what is right. Hatred poisons the soul, blinds the heart, and fills life with bitterness.

Hatred leads to sin and even rebellion against God. It ignores His command to love others and causes people to act against His will. A person who hates enjoys pointing out the faults of others and takes pleasure in their downfall. Whether toward a friend, a brother, or a servant, hatred brings destruction.

Hatred and envy go hand in hand. A hateful person cannot stand to see others succeed and becomes sick with jealousy at the sight of their prosperity. Love, on the other hand, brings healing, even to those who have sinned. But hatred only seeks to destroy and refuses to show mercy, even for the smallest mistakes.

Hatred works alongside Satan, using anger and reckless actions to bring harm. In contrast, the spirit of love follows God's law, leading to patience and salvation. Hatred creates lies and deception, turning small problems into major conflicts. It twists what is good into something evil and fills the heart with rage, violence, and greed. It corrupts everything it touches and leads only to destruction.

I tell you these things from my own experience, so you will reject hatred and hold on to love. Righteousness drives out hatred, and humility destroys jealousy. A just and humble person is ashamed to act unfairly, for he knows God sees his heart.

A person who fears the Lord will not speak against those who are holy. The fear of God removes hatred, for a righteous person does not want to offend the Lord—not even in his thoughts. These are the lessons I learned after repenting for my hatred toward Joseph.

True repentance removes ignorance and reveals the truth. It opens the eyes, fills the soul with wisdom, and leads the mind toward salvation. Through repentance, a person gains understanding, even without instruction, for God speaks to a humble heart.

The Lord punished me for my sins. I suffered from a disease of the liver, and if not for the prayers of my father Jacob, I would have died. A person is punished in the same way he sins. Because I had harbored cruel anger toward Joseph, I endured severe pain in my liver for eleven months—the same amount of time I allowed hatred to rule my heart.

My children, learn from my mistakes. Choose love, righteousness, and humility instead of hatred and envy. Live according to God's commandments, for they will bring you life and peace."

Chapter II.

Gad, the ninth son of Jacob, spoke to his children with wisdom and a sincere heart, urging them to let go of hatred and embrace love. He had learned from experience how destructive hatred could be, and with deep concern, he shared his final words.

"My children, I beg you to love one another as brothers. Remove all hatred from your hearts. Let your love be shown not only in your words and actions but also in your thoughts and feelings. True love must come from within and spread outward, shaping the way you live.

I must confess that, in front of my father, I spoke kindly to Joseph. But as soon as I was away from him, hatred clouded my mind, filling me with thoughts of harming Joseph. Hatred is a poison that sneaks in unnoticed and takes control, turning even good intentions into evil.

Love each other sincerely, my children. If someone wrongs you, go to them in peace and speak to them with kindness. Do not hold grudges or hide bitterness in your heart. If they admit their fault and ask for forgiveness, forgive them without hesitation. Let love and mercy be stronger than anger and resentment.

If they refuse to admit their wrongdoing, do not let anger take over. Avoid arguing or speaking to them in frustration, as this may cause even more hatred. Your anger might lead them to swear or act out in defiance, and in doing so, you will both fall into sin. Keep your heart calm and trust in God's justice instead of taking matters into your own hands.

Be careful not to share your private thoughts or disputes with others, especially in legal matters. If someone overhears and misunderstands your words, they may turn against you. This could create unnecessary conflict and cause them to sin against you. Many people pretend to offer advice or support, but their true motives may be selfish or deceitful.

Even if someone refuses to acknowledge their wrongdoing, but deep down they feel shame when confronted, do not keep pressing them harshly. They may still find the humility to change and avoid repeating their mistakes. If they truly repent, they may even come to respect you, fear God, and seek peace with you.

But if they remain stubborn and continue in their wrongdoing, forgive them anyway. Let your forgiveness come from your heart, freeing yourself from the burden of anger. Do not seek revenge, for judgment belongs to the Lord alone. Trust that He sees everything and will judge fairly.

My children, hatred only brings pain, separation, and destruction. Love, on the other hand, brings healing, unity, and peace. Forgiveness is not just for the one who is forgiven—it also frees the one who forgives. Trust in the Lord's justice, and let love and mercy guide your actions, even when others do wrong.

If you see another man succeed, do not let your heart be troubled or filled with envy. Instead, pray for him with sincerity, asking the Lord to bless him even more. This will not only bring peace to your soul but also help you grow in righteousness.

If he rises to even greater success, do not let jealousy take hold of you. Remember that life on earth is temporary, and in the end, every person faces the same fate. Instead of being envious, be grateful to God, who gives blessings as He sees fit and provides for all according to His wisdom.

Seek to understand God's ways, and you will find peace of mind and rest for your soul. Trust in His justice and His timing, knowing that His ways are greater than ours.

If someone gains wealth through dishonesty, do not envy them, even if their success seems unfair. Look at the example of Esau, my father's brother—he gathered great wealth, but he did not follow righteousness. Be patient and wait for the Lord's judgment, for He sees everything and will act at the right time.

God, in His mercy, may take away wealth that was gained through sin. If the sinner repents, God will forgive him. But if he refuses to change, his punishment will be eternal, and he will lose not only his wealth but also his soul.

A poor man who lives without jealousy, is content with what he has, and pleases the Lord in all things is more blessed than any rich man. He is free from the worries and temptations that trouble those who chase after wealth without seeking righteousness.

So, my children, remove envy from your hearts and replace it with love. Be honest and sincere in all that you do. Jealousy and envy destroy the soul, but love brings peace, unity, and favor with God.

Teach these lessons to your children so they may also walk in the ways of the Lord. Instruct them to respect Judah and Levi, for through their descendants, the Lord will bring salvation to Israel. These two tribes have been chosen by God for His purpose, and their role in His plan is sacred and everlasting.

Yet, I see that in the future, your descendants will turn away from the Lord. They will fall into sin and bring trouble upon themselves. But even then, God's mercy and justice will remain.

I have spoken to you from my heart. Now, I remind you once more—follow your father's teachings, and when my time comes, bury me with our ancestors. Stay true to the traditions and the God of our fathers in everything you do."

When he finished speaking, he lay down peacefully and passed away. Five years later, his sons carried him to Hebron and buried him with his ancestors, just as he had wished.

The Testament of Asher

The Tenth Son of Jacob and Zilpah.

Chapter I.

Asher, the tenth son of Jacob and Zilpah, gathered his children as he neared the end of his life. At 125 years old, while still strong and healthy, he spoke to them with wisdom, sharing the lessons he had learned.

"My sons, listen carefully to your father, for I want to teach you what is right in the eyes of the Lord. God has given people two choices in life—two paths they can follow, two desires within them, two ways of acting, and two possible outcomes. Everything in life has an opposite, and each person must choose which path to take.

There is the way of good and the way of evil. Within every person, there are two forces—one leading toward righteousness and the other toward sin. If a person chooses to follow goodness, their actions will reflect it. Even if they make mistakes, their heart will lead them to repentance, allowing them to correct their ways and turn back to what is right.

But if someone follows the path of evil, their actions will show it. They will reject what is good, embrace sin, and fall under the influence of wickedness. Even when they try to do something good, their corrupted heart twists their actions toward selfishness and harm.

Some people may appear to be doing good, but if their intentions are selfish or dishonest, their actions will ultimately lead to harm. For example, a person may use others for their own benefit, showing no kindness to those who help them commit wrongdoing. Though they may pretend to do good, their actions are still rooted in evil.

Another example is someone who steals, cheats, or takes from others but then gives to the poor as if they are generous. While charity is good, their kindness is spoiled by dishonesty, making their actions sinful before God.

There are also those who live in sin—committing adultery or other immoral acts—while outwardly appearing religious by fasting or following traditions. Though they may seem devoted, their sinful behavior makes their outward acts meaningless.

People like this are like hares—they may look clean on the outside, but they are unclean in reality. God does not accept such double-mindedness. He calls us to be sincere and whole in our righteousness, not living with divided hearts.

So, my children, do not be like those who try to live in both good and evil. Instead, cling only to what is good, for God dwells in those who are sincere and pure in heart. Wickedness, however, pushes God away and invites evil into a person's life. Those who try to live in both worlds are not truly serving God—they are only serving themselves.

People who are committed to goodness may sometimes be misunderstood or falsely accused by those who are double-minded. But in God's eyes, their actions are righteous. Even if it seems like their choices are complicated, their intentions are pure, and they align with God's will.

Some people choose to completely separate themselves from those who do evil, keeping their bodies and souls undefiled. Though their ways may seem extreme, they show true devotion to God.

Everything in life has an opposite. Within wealth, there is greed. In joy, sorrow can hide. Even in marriage, there can be selfish desires. Life leads to death, honor can turn to disgrace, day gives way to night, and light is followed by darkness. Just as these things are connected, so too does eternal life follow death for those who walk in righteousness.

Truth cannot be changed into a lie, and what is right cannot become wrong. Everything is revealed under the light of God. I have lived my life with this understanding, striving to follow the commandments of the Lord with sincerity. I sought out the truth in all things and did my best to live by it.

My children, take these lessons to heart. Follow God's commandments with complete devotion. Those who are double-minded fall into sin twice over—first, by doing wrong themselves, and second, by encouraging others to sin with them. They align themselves with deceitful spirits and work against righteousness.

Remain steadfast in God's law, rejecting evil and holding on to what is good. When your life comes to an end, you will stand before the angels of God and the forces of darkness. Those who lived in wickedness will be tormented by the evil they served, but those who lived in peace will be led by the angel of the Lord into eternal life.

Do not, my children, be like the people of Sodom, who sinned against God's messengers and were destroyed forever. I know that in the future, you will fall into sin and be taken captive by your enemies. Your land will be ruined, your holy places destroyed, and you will be scattered across the earth like water poured out.

But do not lose hope. The Most High will one day visit the earth. He will come as a man, living among people, eating and drinking with them. He will defeat the power of evil and bring salvation to both Israel and the Gentiles. Through Him, God Himself will speak and act as a man.

Pass these teachings on to your children so they will not turn away from the Lord. I know that many of your descendants will fall into corruption, following human traditions instead of God's law. They will be scattered like Gad and Dan, losing their land, their identity, and even their language. But in His mercy, the Lord will gather them back together through faith, for the sake of Abraham, Isaac, and Jacob.

After saying these things, Asher instructed his sons to bury him in Hebron. Then, he lay down peacefully, passed away, and was buried by his sons alongside his ancestors, just as he had requested.

The Testament of Joseph

The Eleventh Son of Jacob and Rachel.

Chapter I.

Joseph, the eleventh son of Jacob and Rachel, was known for his wisdom, perseverance, and unshakable faith in God. Despite facing betrayal, hardship, and temptation, he remained true to his values. As his life neared its end, he gathered his sons and brothers to share his story and offer them guidance.

"My brothers and my dear children, listen carefully to my words. I, Joseph, was deeply loved by Israel, yet my life was filled with challenges. Let me tell you about my journey, one that tested my faith but was upheld by the truth of the Lord.

Throughout my life, I faced jealousy and even threats against my life. But I never turned away from righteousness. My brothers despised me, but the Lord loved me. They plotted to kill me, yet the God of my fathers protected me. They threw me into a pit, but the Most High lifted me out. I was sold as a slave, yet the Lord set me free.

Though I was taken captive, God's mighty hand rescued me. When I suffered from hunger, He provided for me. When I was alone, He comforted me. In sickness, He healed me. When I was imprisoned, He showed me favor and broke my chains. Though I was falsely accused, He defended me. When the Egyptians spoke against me, the Lord delivered me. Even when other servants envied me, God lifted me up.

Pharaoh's chief officer trusted me and placed me in charge of his household. Everything he owned was under my care. But while I was responsible for all his affairs, I faced my greatest test—the relentless temptation of his wife, who tried to lead me into sin. Yet the God of Israel, the God of my fathers, saved me from falling into that trap.

Even though I resisted her, she had me thrown into prison. I was beaten and humiliated. But the Lord, in His mercy, made me find favor with the prison keeper. No matter how dark my situation seemed, He never abandoned me. Those who fear the Lord are never truly alone—not in trouble, not in chains, not in suffering, and not even in their worst moments.

God is not like humans—He does not grow weak or afraid. He never changes, and His strength supports all who trust in Him. Sometimes, He steps back for a while to test the heart and strengthen the soul. He tested me ten times, and in each trial, I remained faithful. For patience brings great rewards, and endurance leads to countless blessings.

Many times, the Egyptian woman threatened my life. She had me punished, only to later call me back and try again. When I refused her, she tried to persuade me with promises, saying, 'If you give in to me, you will rule over my household. You will have everything my husband owns.'

But I remembered my father's teachings. I ran to my room, wept, and prayed to the Lord. For seven years, I fasted and sought His help. Even though I lived in luxury in the eyes of the Egyptians, inside, I was crying out to God. Those who fast for the Lord are given strength and radiance as a blessing.

When my master was away, I avoided drinking wine. Often, I went three days without eating, giving my food to the poor and sick instead. Every morning, I woke early to pray and grieve over the woman's sinful ways. She would even visit me at night, pretending to care for me.

At first, she acted like a mother, saying she had no children and saw me as a son. I believed her at first and allowed her kindness. But soon, her true intentions became clear—she wanted to lead me into sin. When I realized her deceit, my heart ached for her, and I prayed for many days.

I tried to teach her about the Most High, hoping she would change her ways. But instead of listening, she flattered me, calling me righteous and holy. In front of her husband, she praised my good character, but in private, she tried to trap me with her words.

Through all of this, the Lord gave me strength. Remember, my children, always put your trust in God. He is faithful and will protect those who honor Him, even in the hardest of trials.

She even tried to convince me by saying, 'Do not be afraid of my husband—he trusts you completely. Even if someone accused you, he would never believe it.' She used these words to tempt me, but they only brought me more pain.

I fell to the ground, crying out to God, begging Him to save me from her deception and keep me from sinning. No matter how many times she tried, she could not break me.

Frustrated, she changed her approach. She came to me again, pretending she wanted to learn about God. She claimed she was ready to leave behind her idols and even said she would convince her husband to do the same if I agreed to be with her.

She disguised her temptation as something righteous, but I saw through her lies. I answered, 'The Lord calls His people to remain pure. He does not accept those who commit adultery. Only those who come before Him with clean hearts and truthful words are pleasing in His sight.'"

Even after everything I said, she remained silent, still scheming to get what she wanted. I dedicated myself even more to fasting and prayer, asking the Lord to protect me from her advances. Then one day, she came to me again and said, "If you refuse to be with me, I will poison my husband and make you my spouse."

Horrified, I tore my clothes and said, "Have fear of God! Do not do something so wicked! You will only bring destruction upon yourself. I will tell everyone about your evil plan." Terrified that I would expose her, she begged me to stay silent.

To win me over, she started sending me gifts and offering me luxuries, trying to tempt me into changing my mind. Then, in desperation, she even tried to use magic against me, mixing enchantments into my food in an attempt to bewitch me.

When her servant brought the food to me, I looked up and saw a vision—an angel handing me a sword along with the meal. I immediately realized that she was trying to deceive me again. As soon as the servant left, I wept bitterly and refused to eat the food she had sent.

The next day, she came to me and asked, "Why haven't you eaten the food I sent?"

I answered, "Because it was poisoned with evil. You told me you wanted to turn away from idolatry and serve the Lord, but your actions show the opposite. The God of my fathers has revealed your wickedness to me through His angel. I kept this knowledge to myself, hoping you would repent."

To show her the power of God, I said, "The evil plans of the wicked cannot harm those who truly serve the Lord. Watch, and I will eat this food before you to prove it." Before taking a bite, I prayed, "O God of my fathers and angel of Abraham, be with me now." Then, I ate.

Seeing this, she fell to the ground, weeping at my feet. I lifted her up and warned her once again to turn away from her sin. She promised she wouldn't do anything evil again, but I could tell her heart was still filled with wickedness. She immediately began looking for another way to trap me.

Her frustration grew, and she pretended to be sick, sighing and moaning to get attention.

When her husband noticed her troubled expression, he asked, "What is wrong? Why do you look so sad?"

She answered, "I feel pain in my heart, and my spirit is heavy." Believing her, he comforted her, not realizing she was lying.

Then, when her husband was away, she came to me again, in a desperate state, and said, "If you do not lie with me, I will take my own life! I will hang myself or throw myself off a cliff."

I saw that she had completely lost control, and that the spirit of Beliar had taken over her thoughts. Distressed, I prayed to the Lord for guidance and strength. Then I turned to her and said, "Why are you in such torment? Why do you let sin blind you? Have you not thought about your children, your future, or what will happen because of your actions? If you take your life, Asteho, your husband's concubine, will mistreat your children and erase your memory from the earth."

Hearing this, she said, "So you do care for me! That alone gives me comfort. If you are willing to look after me and my children, I can accept that for now and hope that one day, my desires will be fulfilled."

But I knew she was still thinking wickedly, twisting my words to fit her own desires.

I did not speak to her out of love but out of obedience to the Lord. When someone is controlled by sinful passion, even the smallest act of kindness is misunderstood and used to fuel their wickedness. Even though I tried to reason with her, she left around midday, still set on getting what she wanted.

I fell to my knees and prayed to the Lord without stopping, crying out to Him all day and night, asking for deliverance from her constant pursuit.

At sunrise, I was still praying and pleading for help.

Then, in her desperation, she made one final attempt. She grabbed my robe and tried to force me to be with her. She held onto my clothes tightly, refusing to let go. Seeing that she would not stop, I pulled away, leaving my robe in her hands. I fled, naked and ashamed, but determined to stay pure.

Enraged and humiliated, she clutched my robe and accused me of attacking her.

When her husband returned, he believed her lies. In his anger, he had me locked in his household prison. The next day, he had me beaten and then sent to Pharaoh's prison.

Even in my suffering, I gave thanks to the Lord. I sang His praises, even in the darkness of my cell. I was filled with joy because God had saved me from falling into sin.

The woman, however, was filled with guilt and sadness. She would visit me in prison and send messages, saying, "If you give in to me now, I will have you released from these chains."

But I never even considered her offer, not even in my thoughts, because I knew it was against the Lord's will.

God values those who remain pure, even in difficult circumstances, more than those who live in luxury but sin. He rewards those who stay faithful and resist temptation. If someone stays righteous and seeks glory for the right reasons, the Most High will honor them in His time.

Many times, even when she was unwell, she would come to my prison, pretending to listen to my prayers. She sighed and moaned, hoping I would change my mind, but I stayed silent.

When I was still in her house, she made bold attempts to tempt me. She dressed in fine clothes, revealing her arms, legs, and chest, using her beauty to try to seduce me. But the Lord, in His mercy, protected me from her tricks. He guarded my heart and body, keeping me from falling into sin.

Chapter II.

Joseph faced many challenges because of a cunning and deceitful woman in Egypt. If you want to see an interesting prophecy, read verses 73 and 74.

My dear children, patience, prayer, and fasting have incredible power. They can change both your heart and your situation. I urge you to stay pure and disciplined, praying and fasting with a humble spirit. When you do this, God will be with you, because He loves those who are pure in heart.

No matter what struggles you face—whether it's jealousy, hardship, or false accusations—God will protect and lift up those who remain pure. He did this for me, and He will do the same for anyone who walks in His ways.

My brothers knew that our father loved me dearly, but I never became proud. Even as a child, I feared God and understood that worldly things do not last forever. I never tried to take revenge on my brothers. When they sold me as a slave, I didn't tell the Ishmaelites that I was the son of Jacob, a powerful man, because I wanted to protect my brothers' honor.

Let this be a lesson to you, my children: always fear God in everything you do, and respect your brothers no matter what happens. Whoever follows God's ways and keeps His commandments will be loved by Him.

When the Ishmaelites took me to a foreign land, they asked if I was a slave. To avoid disgracing my brothers, I told them that I was. One of their elders doubted my words, saying I didn't look like a slave, but I stuck to my story.

When we reached Egypt, they argued about who would buy me. In the end, they agreed to leave me with a merchant until they returned. God gave me favor with this merchant, and he trusted me with his entire household. Because of me, God blessed him, increasing his wealth and prosperity. I stayed with him for a little over three months, and during that time, God continued to bless everything around me.

One day, the wife of Pentephris, a powerful official of Pharaoh, heard about me. She was curious and told her husband about me, saying that I had brought prosperity to the merchant. She suggested that Pentephris take me into his household, believing that my presence would bring them blessings as well.

Pentephris listened to his wife and accused the merchant of kidnapping me from Canaan. The merchant, terrified, fell at his feet and pleaded for mercy, saying he had only been taking care of me until the Ishmaelites returned. Still, Pentephris had him beaten.

Then, Pentephris called for me. I showed him respect because of his high position. He asked if I was a slave or a free man. I told him the truth—I was a slave purchased by the Ishmaelites in Canaan. But he didn't believe me and had me beaten as well.

While I was being punished, the official's wife watched from a window and sent a message to her husband, saying that his judgment was unfair. She argued that I was clearly a free man and had been wrongly enslaved. But Pentephris decided to keep me in prison until the Ishmaelites returned to confirm my story. His wife, however, had another reason for wanting me free—she desired me for herself, though I didn't fully understand her intentions at the time.

After twenty-four days, the Ishmaelites came back. They had learned about my father's sorrow and asked why I had claimed to be a slave when I was really the son of a great man in Canaan. Their words deeply hurt me. I wanted to cry, but I held back my tears so I wouldn't bring shame upon my brothers. Even though I was suffering, I trusted in God's plan.

The Ishmaelites decided to sell me to avoid getting in trouble with my father, Jacob. They feared his power, knowing he was both strong and favored by God. Meanwhile, the merchant, afraid of being punished, asked the Ishmaelites to clear him of guilt. They asked me to say that they had bought me with money so they wouldn't be blamed.

At the same time, the wife of Pentephris urged her husband to buy me. She even sent her servant to purchase me from the Ishmaelites. However, they demanded a high price. Determined, she sent another servant with instructions to pay whatever was needed to get me. The servant eventually bought me for eighty pieces of gold but lied to his mistress, saying he had paid one hundred. I knew about the lie, but I kept quiet to protect him.

You see, my children, all the hardship I endured just to protect my brothers from shame. So, I urge you to love one another sincerely and be patient with each other's mistakes. God takes joy in brothers who love and support each other.

When my brothers later came to Egypt, they found that I had secretly returned the money they had given for food. I did not punish them; instead, I comforted them. Even after our father Jacob passed away, I loved my brothers even more. I carried out my father's wishes with great care, and I made sure my brothers never lacked anything.

I treated their children as my own, and my own children served them. Their happiness was my happiness, and their pain was my pain. I shared everything I had with them and never acted as if I was above them, despite my high position. Instead, I lived as their equal.

So, my children, if you follow God's commandments, He will bless and lift you up. If others try to hurt you, do good to them instead and pray for them. God will rescue you from harm.

Look at my life—I was blessed because of humility and patience. I married Asenath, the daughter of an Egyptian priest, and received great wealth. But I remained humble. God continued to bless me, keeping me strong and healthy even in old age. In many ways, I resembled my father, Jacob.

Now, listen to a vision I had. I saw twelve deer eating together. Nine scattered across the earth, while three remained. Then, from Judah came a young woman wearing fine linen. She gave birth to a spotless lamb, and a lion stood beside it. Many wild animals tried to attack the lamb, but it defeated them all. Because of this lamb, both people and angels rejoiced, and the whole earth was filled with joy.

This vision will come true in the future. So, my children, follow God's commandments and honor Levi and Judah, for from them will come the Lamb of God. He will take away the sins of the world and bring salvation to everyone, both Israel and other nations. His kingdom will last forever, unlike mine, which was only temporary.

I know that after my death, the Egyptians will oppress you. But God will bring justice and lead you to the land He promised to our ancestors. When you leave Egypt, take my bones with you. When you do, God's light will be with you, while darkness will remain with the Egyptians.

Bury your mother, Asenath, near Rachel's resting place. After saying these words, Joseph lay down, stretched out his feet, and peacefully passed away at a good old age.

All of Israel mourned for Joseph, and even the Egyptians grieved with them. When the Israelites left Egypt, they carried Joseph's bones and buried him in Hebron, with his ancestors. Joseph lived to be 110 years old.

The Testament of Benjamin

The Twelfth Son of Jacob and Rachel.

Chapter I.

Benjamin, the youngest son of Jacob and Rachel, grew up to be a wise and kind man.

Before he passed away at the age of 125, he gathered his children, kissed them, and shared his final words:

"I was born when my father, Jacob, was very old, just as Isaac was born to Abraham in his old age. Sadly, my mother, Rachel, died giving birth to me, so I never got to drink her milk. Instead, her servant Bilhah nursed me and cared for me as her own child.

For twelve years after Joseph was born, my mother could not have more children. But she prayed to God with all her heart, fasting for twelve days, and He answered her prayers—she became pregnant and gave birth to me. My father had always wanted Rachel to have two sons, and when I was born, he named me Benjamin, meaning 'son of days,' because I was the answer to his prayers.

When I traveled to Egypt and met my brother Joseph, he recognized me and asked, 'What did our brothers tell our father when they sold me?' I answered, 'They dipped your coat in blood and sent it to him, saying, "Look at this and see if it belongs to your son."' Joseph then told me, 'When they took my coat, they sold me to the Ishmaelites. They gave me only a loincloth, whipped me, and made me run. But later, one of the men who beat me was killed by a lion, and the others were terrified.'

So, my children, I urge you to love and obey the Lord, the Creator of heaven and earth. Follow the example of Joseph, who was a good and righteous man. If your heart is focused on doing what is right, you will see things clearly. Love God and be kind to others. Even if evil forces try to harm you, they will not succeed—just as they could not defeat Joseph.

Think about how many people wanted to hurt Joseph, but God protected him. Those who love God and care for others are safe from evil plans. No enemy, whether human or animal, can destroy them because the Lord is their protector.

Joseph even prayed for our father to forgive his brothers for their cruelty. Jacob, deeply moved, embraced Joseph, kissed him, and wept for a long time. Then he spoke of the future, saying, 'Through you, my son, a great prophecy will be fulfilled. A sinless one will be sacrificed for the sake of sinners. His blood will bring salvation to both Israel and other nations. He will defeat evil and those who serve it.'

My children, do you see what happens to a good and righteous person? Follow his example so you, too, can receive rewards in heaven. A good person does not give in to jealousy or hatred. He is kind to everyone, even those who do wrong. If others try to harm him, he responds with goodness, knowing that God is his shield. He treats the righteous as if they were his own family. He is not jealous of the wealthy or envious of those who succeed. Instead, he admires those who are strong and virtuous. He helps the poor, shows compassion to the weak, and praises God with joy.

A kind-hearted person loves others who have a noble spirit as if they were his own soul. If you live this way, even wicked people will treat you with kindness. Your goodness may inspire the unjust to change their ways. Those who are greedy may learn to be generous. When you act righteously, even evil spirits will flee from you, and wild animals will fear you. Darkness cannot overpower a person filled with goodness and light.

If someone harms a righteous man, they will regret it because a righteous man does not seek revenge. Even when betrayed, he prays for the one who wronged him. He may suffer for a time, but in the end, he will be lifted up—just like Joseph. A good man does not fall for the tricks of evil, because the angel of peace guides him. He does not focus on worldly riches or chase after pleasure. He does not harm others or desire things that belong to them. His greatest treasure is the Lord, and he finds joy in Him alone.

A good heart does not waver between kindness and cruelty, truth and lies, or love and hatred. It is pure and steady, loving all people equally. Such a person does not seek human praise or fear human rejection, for God is their true home, and His light fills their soul.

So, my children, always strive to have good and noble hearts. Obey the Lord's commandments with all your strength. Stay away from dishonesty, hatred, and falsehood. Instead, live with purity and love for everyone. By doing so, you will reflect God's image, and His peace will always be with you.

A righteous person keeps his mind pure so that neither people nor God can find fault with him. In contrast, evil people are full of lies and deceit, always changing their minds and never acting with honesty.

This is why, my children, I urge you to stay far away from evil. Those who follow wickedness may feel powerful for a time, but it will only lead to destruction. It brings seven great troubles: first, it corrupts the mind; then it leads to violence, ruin, suffering, exile, hunger, fear, and ultimately, complete destruction.

This is why God punished Cain seven times over, for he was guilty of great evil. Every hundred years, God sent a plague upon him. His suffering began when he was two hundred years old, and by the time he reached nine hundred, his life came to an end.

This was God's judgment for Cain's sin against his brother Abel. In the same way, Lamech, who committed similar sins, was punished seventy times seven. Let this be a lesson: those who hold onto jealousy and hatred, like Cain did, will face God's judgment forever."

Chapter II.

The third verse gives a clear and down-to-earth example of how the ancient patriarchs spoke.

Now, my children, I encourage you to stay away from evil actions, jealousy, and hatred toward your brothers. Instead, fill your hearts with goodness and love. Let love guide your thoughts and actions in everything you do.

A person with a pure heart and a mind full of love will not look at a woman with lustful thoughts. Such a person remains pure, for God's Spirit lives within them. Just like the sun can shine on dirt without being stained but instead dries it up and removes the bad smell, a pure heart stays clean even when surrounded by a sinful world.

According to the words of the righteous Enoch, I know that evil will rise among you. Many will fall into sin, following the ways of Sodom, and they will be destroyed—except for a small group who remain faithful. Many will return to sinful ways with women, and because of this, the kingdom of God will be taken away from them.

Still, the temple of God will remain among you, and in the future, there will be a final temple that will be even more glorious than the first. The twelve tribes will gather there, along with many people from other nations. This will continue until the Most High sends His salvation through His one and only prophet. This prophet will enter the first temple, where He will be rejected and treated with great dishonor. He will be lifted up on a tree, and the temple veil will tear apart. Then, God's Spirit will come upon the Gentiles like fire.

This prophet will rise from the dead and ascend into heaven. I know that He will live humbly on earth, yet rule with great glory in heaven.

When Joseph was in Egypt, I deeply wished to see him. Through the prayers of our father Jacob, God granted me a vision of Joseph's face during the day, showing me exactly how he looked.

After saying these things, he turned to his children and said, "My dear children, my time to leave this world has come. So, live in truth, be honest with one another, and follow the Lord's laws and commandments. These are the most valuable treasures I leave for you. Pass them on to your children, just as Abraham, Isaac, and Jacob passed them down to us.

They taught us to remain faithful to God's commands until the time when the Lord brings salvation to all nations. Then, you will see Enoch, Noah, Shem, Abraham, Isaac, and Jacob rise again in joy and stand at God's right hand.

On that day, we will rise again and lead our tribes in worshiping the King of heaven, who came to earth as a humble man. Those who believe in Him will rejoice with Him.

All people will rise—some to honor and others to shame. The Lord will judge Israel first because, when He came to save them, they did not believe in Him. Then, He will judge the Gentiles who also refused to believe in Him when He walked among them. Israel will be held accountable through the faith of the Gentiles, just as Esau was judged through the Midianites. These deceivers led their own brothers into sin and idolatry, causing them to turn away from God instead of joining those who truly fear the Lord.

But if you, my children, live in holiness and obey God's commandments, we will be together again, and all of Israel will be gathered to the Lord. I will no longer be known as a wild and greedy wolf because of past mistakes, but as a servant of God who provides for those who do good.

In the last days, someone greatly loved by God will rise from the tribes of Judah and Levi. He will carry out God's will and bring new knowledge that will enlighten the Gentiles. Until the end of time, his words and deeds will be remembered like a beautiful song among the Gentiles and their rulers. His life and works will be written in the holy books, and he will remain God's chosen servant forever.

He will walk among the tribes, fulfilling what is missing, just as my father Jacob prophesied. After saying these words, he lay back, stretched out his feet, and peacefully passed away in a calm and beautiful sleep.

His sons honored his last wishes, carrying his body to Hebron and burying him with his ancestors. He lived for a total of one hundred and twenty-five years.

Thank You for Reading

Dear Reader,

We hope this timeless classic has sparked your imagination and enriched your literary journey. Now that you've turned the final page, we want to share a vision for the future of reading—one where every classic you've ever wanted to explore is at your fingertips, in a format that best suits your life.

We'd like to invite you to gain immediate, unlimited digital & audiobook access to hundreds of the most treasured literary classics ever written—along with the option to secure deluxe paperback, hardcover & box set editions at printing cost. Together, we can spark a new global literary renaissance alongside our small, independent publishing house called "The Library of Alexandria."

Thousands of years ago, the Library of Alexandria stood as a beacon of knowledge—until it was lost to history. We aim to reignite that spirit of preservation and discovery right now, in the modern age—only this time, it's accessible to all, in every language and every format.

Picture a world where every timeless classic, novel, poem, or philosophical treatise is not only available to read but also updated for today's readers—modernized, translated into any language or dialect, and ready to enjoy in any format you choose, whether that is in an eBook, audiobook, paperback, or deluxe hardcover & box set version a printing cost.

By joining our movement to rebuild the modern Library of Alexandria, you become part of an unprecedented mission to offer:

- **Unlimited Audiobook & eBook Access to the Greatest Classics of All Time**

Instantly explore thousands of legendary works, from Plato and Shakespeare to Jane Austen and Leo Tolstoy. All are instantly ready to read or listen to, giving you a complete literary universe at your fingertips.

- **Paperback & Deluxe Editions at Printing Costs:**

Purchase any title in a paperback, deluxe hardbound, or deluxe boxset edition at printing costs, shipped right to your doorstep. Curate your personal library of Alexandria with editions worthy of display—crafted to last, designed to captivate, and delivered straight to your door.

- **Modern translations for Contemporary Readers in all languages and dialects**

Discover a vast selection of classics reimagined in clear, current language—no more struggling with outdated phrases or obscure references. Next to the original versions, we aim to offer translations in as many languages and dialects as possible.

As we continue our translation efforts and add new languages, readers everywhere can connect with these works as if they were written today. By bridging linguistic divides, you're contributing to ensuring that these timeless stories become more meaningful, accessible, and inspiring for people across the globe.

- **Your Personal Library of Alexandria:**

Over the months and years, you'll curate a unique physical archive of classics—each volume a testament to your taste, curiosity, and love of knowledge. It's not just about owning books—it's about curating a cultural legacy you'll cherish and pass down for generations to come.

- **Join a Global Literary Renaissance:**

  Your support fuels an ongoing mission: allowing us to reinvest in offering deluxe print editions (including special boxsets) at their true cost, broaden the range of available formats and translations, and extend the reach of these works to new audiences worldwide. By joining today, you're not just preserving a legacy of masterpieces; you set in motion a powerful wave of literary accessibility.

  We are more than a publisher—we're a movement, and we can't do it alone. Your support lets us scale our mission, preserving and reimagining history's greatest works for tomorrow's readers.

Become a Torchbearer of knowledge.

Thank you for picking up this book and allowing us into your literary journey. As you turn the pages, know that you're part of something larger: a global effort to keep these stories alive, share their wisdom across borders and generations, and spark a true cultural revival for the modern era.

If this resonates with you—please consider taking the next step by visiting:

www.libraryofalexandria.com

With gratitude and a shared love of knowledge,

The Modern Library of Alexandria Team

Visit:

www.libraryofalexandria.com

Or scan the code below:

www.ingramcontent.com/pod-product-compliance
Lightning Source LLC
Chambersburg PA
CBHW010236100426
42813CB00011B/2634

9 781804 217641